SMALL TOWN SCANDAL

A REAL LIFE LOVE LESSON

RESIA NANK

outskirts
press

Outskirts Press, Inc.
http://www.outskirtspress.com

ISBN: 978-1-4787-7609-3

Outskirts Press and the "OP" logo are trademarks belonging to Outskirts Press, Inc.

PRINTED IN THE UNITED STATES OF AMERICA

Preface

Sometimes the universe, or fate, or God, or whatever name you give the force that sweeps our lives forward, puts unbelievable coincidences in our path or presents serendipitous circumstances that cannot be explained other than by faith. The tale and all of the incidents depicted are true – the secret is out!

Names have been changed to protect those involved. If all of this happened to one of us, just think of how many stories we 70-plus million baby boomers have yet to tell.

DEDICATION

To all the old friends who put up with my youthful antics: I came in like a hurricane and left damage in my wake. I'm sorry if I hurt anyone along the way.

And, to all my newer friends who listened to me talk about this book for more than 10 years, thanks for your patience and your feedback.

Special thanks to Robin Castillo and Adolfo Santibanez of Studio Via for the cover image and to my dear friend and book editor, Donna Foley.

TABLE OF CONTENTS

Chapter 1

THE PLAN B STRATEGY

I WAS THE one who always knew what she wanted, being determined to find a way to get it. Other teens wondered, "What will I be when I grow up?" Not me. I always had a goal. And if I couldn't get it, I always had a Plan B.

This theory applied to all areas of my life: career, lovers, possessions, and family.

Example: In high school, I obstinately told the guidance counselor that I didn't need Chemistry mucking up my GPA because I was going to be an actress. The Friday pop quizzes on the metric system were killing me! I offered to take Advanced Biology instead but was rejected for lack of the Chemistry credit, then relegated to the Journalism class. In Journalism, I thrived. I had some talent for writing and huge ambitions. I decided, once chosen to succeed Shelly Dean as editor of the school pages of the community newspaper, that this could be an acceptable career option if the acting thing didn't pan out. Broadcast journalists were on TV, after all.

But, this was not my first foray into the Plan B strategy of life. At the age of five, my incessant whining of the word "pony" drove my mother to leave me for long periods with my grandparents. Pop and I scoured the back roads of three counties in search of equine companionship, me standing on the front bench seat of his pickup. I knew Pop was a soft touch, and I knew I would eventually get a pony.

On the day his truck finally arrived with a brown pony in the back, I cried my eyes out. I was crushed. Had he not heard me? That pony was brown, and not the beautiful, golden palomino I had requested. I told him to take it back. (Remember, I was five. After this incident I learned not to shoot myself in the foot!) My strategy for playing parents against grandparents to get what I wanted perfected itself soon after the pony fiasco. I also learned to apply it as a Plan B between my mother and my birth father from whom she was divorced when I was two.

As for lovers, until I was in my third marriage, I never worked without a net. Yes, I was one of those girls you love to hate (and there were plenty of haters). I always had another potential boyfriend waiting in the wings or a well-heeled "friend with benefits" to take my mind off the situation until a new boyfriend came along. The revolving door was always swinging, owing I suppose to my blond and busty looks and boundless energy to look for men, then put up with them all at once.

Chapter 2

THE ROAD OUT OF POVERTY

BEING SPOILED AS a child, I had no idea until I hit puberty that my family was a statistic—we lived below the national government's poverty level. We had a house and always had more than one car. I had a bicycle, stereo, radio, TV and clothes – all essential for teenaged contentedness. Food was in plentiful supply, but extras for luxury items had to come from my grandparents or my birth father. I knew money was always tight, but I didn't feel poor. I also had a resourcefulness and determination that allowed me to find a way to get the things I wanted.

There was no money saved for college. Still, I would find a way – if not to attend the American Academy of Dramatic Arts, where I longed to study acting but feared living in the Big Apple – then at least a reputable college. By the time I would really need it, there'd be free money from the government's Basic Educational Opportunity Grant (thanks, President Jimmy Carter) to anyone with brains, patience for piles of paperwork and a low-income qualification. I would easily qualify for the BEOG at an in-state university. If I wanted to go out of state, or to acting school, I would have to look harder for an avenue.

The reality of living in poverty consumed me when I discovered while completing college applications how little my parents really earned. The questions rolled in my mind: A grant or scholarship would be great, but how will I live? Pay for books? Eat?

I could work, of course, but that would never keep me in the style to which I had become accustomed at the expense of everyone else in the family. I had to think bigger and keep my eyes open for any and all possible routes to my dream life. Little did I know that as with many best-laid plans, my life would not become the dream I expected. Something, or in my case someone, was about to swoop in and change everything.

Let's start at the beginning.

Chapter 3

A New World of Opportunity on the Stoop

The neighborhood where my family and I lived was small. Our modest brick home was set at the back of a horseshoe-shaped road and was one of only about twenty or so built in this new rural development surrounded by farms. Our half-acre backyard was green and sloped gradually down to a wooded stream. Just through the trees you could see Farmer Holt's cornfield. It was late spring of 1973 and the corn was peeking through the earth in its quest to eclipse the horizon.

The open field to our left was sprouting with dandelions and weeds. It smelled like a great summer in the making.

For my fourteenth birthday on April 8, I lived the fantasy of nearly every pubescent girl by attending a David Cassidy concert. Throngs of screaming teenagers packed the Baltimore Civic Center to see the white-jumpsuited heartthrob prance around and warble. I enjoyed all the hubbub and relished his poster plastered on my bedroom wall.

I also had wheedled my own phone line out of my birth father. It was easy because he felt guilty for the divorce and for seeing me so little while he lived only sixteen miles away. For a fourteen year old to have her own phone – and number – in her own room, was a privilege normally reserved for the elite and was extremely uncommon on Maryland's Eastern Shore at this time.

No one had a cell phone; in fact, we had never seen one. It wasn't until 1976, in a suitcase on an episode of *Charlie's Angels*, when I learned of their existence. Lack of money didn't stop my relatives from spoiling me. The phone was another crucial ingredient in my perfect summer recipe.

My after-school activities had recently been upgraded from mounting my mini-bike to race to the stable where my third pony was kept, (After years of begging, I eventually got a pony at age 11, in spite of sending back the first one for being brown and the second one for being too young to ride.), to simply mounting my new, faster dirt bike for the trails where hoof prints had given way to tire tracks. My bright blue Honda SL70 could send me speeding at least 15 mph faster than my old mini-bike. Learning the clutch was a struggle that ended with a broken taillight, but I eventually got the hang of it.

On this particularly sunny day, as I spun gravel out our driveway, a moving truck was backing into the driveway of the house adjacent to ours. I coasted along the side of the road to get a better view.

My cutoff hip-hugger jean shorts cut into my thighs as I planted my feet on the ground. Parked in front of the moving truck was the coolest party van my teenage eyes had ever seen. Some would have called it psyche-delic. On reflection, the 1972 Dodge van had more of an overlapping rectangular pattern of varied deep tone colors – gold and burgundy - over a dark blue back-ground and no side windows. The exterior made the interior that much more mysterious. We did not have vehicles like this in Easton, let alone in Stoneybrook.

My curiosity piqued, I circled the moving truck and stopped between it and the large lilac bush in the new neighbor's front yard. I watched as a short, very tan man in his early thirties exited the van and opened the back doors, unloading a large motorcycle. He had collar-length, wavy brown hair and his knee-length,

Wrangler cut-offs, a logoed T-shirt and sandals said this is no stuffy businessman. "Wow! Our new neighbors are cool," I thought. Being cool was very important in the seventies and people over thirty generally did not qualify.

"Uh, oh!" He saw me. As I clicked the bike into gear to take off, he waved. I froze. Smiling, he grabbed his gigantic motocross racer and rolled it toward me. The red and blue lettering on his T-shirt read, "Top Gear." I later learned that was his employer; he sold parts and accessories to bike shops. As we introduced ourselves I felt a rising excitement inside me. I could hardly contain it.

This 32-year-old man, Cookie Stephens, was unlike anyone I had ever met. He wasn't exactly handsome; his looks were an odd mix of traits — rough like Ian McShane, sensitive like Dudley Moore, and confident like Bill Bixby — and he had a charismatic way of relating to people. Maybe that's why he was in sales. He didn't seem to care at all what anyone else thought of him. He just was; like a wild mustang no one would harness.

After talking for a few minutes, my excitement waned as I found out he was a friend of my stepfather, Robert. He also had a six-year-old daughter, Shea. He asked if I babysat. I lied and said I regularly did. I guess having two-year-old twin brothers could make anyone hate to babysit. There was truly only one child

I baby-sat – ever. He was a sweet, tow-headed five-year-old boy whose parents owned the best stereo system in the neighborhood and paid well. He was obedient, went to bed on time and slept like a rock while I kara-oked to the Carpenters for hours. Compared to that, sitting for my brothers was another level of hell.

Cookie and I chatted for a long while and I found that he knew a lot of things about our town. Even though he had moved back to Easton from Tennessee, he knew everyone in the local motorcycle shop and he had gone to high school with most of them, including my step dad. The shop was called D & D Honda and was owned by a man named Sidney Dickson. He had recently recruited me on my shiny new SL70 to be in a series of newspaper ads, as Miss D&D Honda, complete with sequined tiara.

Every day after our first encounter, as I cruised down Parker's farm lane, I could not get Cookie out of my head. He was charming and mystifying and I wanted to share in the excitement that I perceived to be his life.

Word spread fast of our cool new neighbor and soon a new evening ritual was born. Female teenagers from the neighborhood, clad in hot pants, midriff tops and hair yarn, would flock to his front stoop to talk and play hand games with Cookie. We were enthralled with being treated like adults while still being allowed to act like kids. The boys were not as especially charmed and soon found other interests.

Marcia, the redheaded Stoneybrook firebrand, and I fought over everything including whom he liked better. I had a leg-up since I had a motorcycle that I rode with Cookie now and then. She also owed me the favor of looking the other way with Cookie because the previous year, Marcia had a fling with a thrice-failed hippy boy whom her parents detested. I had been grounded for enlisting my friend Shelly's brother Bill to provide a locale that enabled her trysts with him. It was a devious plan to escape out the back door of the movie theater and walk to Bill's dad's apartment, then return to be picked up from the theater in just under two hours. Bill and I drank while Marcia and Jim did whatever they did. The problem was Marcia's mother who was suspicious and followed us. It didn't end well for either of us.

Cookie's sales job afforded him lots of free time to play and he became our regular entertainment. In the days when there were three television networks, a fuzzy UHF signal and no Internet, kids played outside all day without fear of abduction and parents rarely worried about our safety or arrest.

On the stoop, we were interrupted occasionally by Cookie's wife, Leona. Some said she was a bitch and others just thought she was jealous of all the attention we received.

I was unsure how my relationship with Leona would unfold. Mom had become fast friends with her but Leona always tried to befriend the younger set. I went shopping with her and Mom one day when maxi halter dresses were in vogue the first time around. After I convinced Mom to allow me to buy one in white, complete with matching plastic dangling hoop earrings, Leona paraded out of the fitting room wearing the same dress in yellow. It was fun and I didn't mind much since she also masterminded a plan to wear our new dresses to Busch's seafood restaurant for dinner the next night.

All dolled up anticipating the sunset, Mom, Leona and I piled into Cookie's van with him and Robert, then headed northwest to the Bay Bridge. The inside of the van was well appointed with soft shag carpet, four leather seats and a removable bunk in the back. At six, Shea was too young for such a long night out so another neighborhood babysitter took my place that evening. I was excited because Busch's was famous for its lobster tank. I planned to order the biggest lobster in it. Although I grew up around seafood I had never tasted the costly delicacy. Most of our seafood meals were crabs, oysters and fish caught by local watermen who gave away some of their catch to friends. Robert would pretend his income could keep up with Cookie's for this one night, so the lobsters didn't stand a chance.

We were having a good time. It didn't seem the least

bit odd that I was out to dinner at a grown up place with two married couples. I preferred being treated as an adult. After a fruit cocktail appetizer, I devoured a nearly three pound lobster, then finished off the rest of Mom's stuffed tail.

As the adults consumed more alcohol, Leona became more and more competitive for Cookie's attention but no one seemed to notice the undercurrent that was building between us, or the footsie we played under the table. How our flirty glances went unnoticed baffled me, but I knew something was brewing.

The ride home was interesting since all the lobster I had stuffed into my gut was causing me a bit of carsickness. Reclining in the back of the van, I daydreamed of what it would be like to be with Cookie, wondering if his thoughts were on me. In spite of the nausea, it was a terrific diversion and the beginning of my life's first grand adventure.

Chapter 4

THE ACCIDENT

A WEEK OR more later I was listening to the radio, singing and feeling the early summer breezes flap through the sheer cotton curtains. It was about four in the afternoon when a thunderous knock came at our front door. I ran and flung it open to find Cookie, bandaged from head to toe, on crutches, and clutching his motorcycle helmet that he had used as a knocker. The helmet was split down the middle.

"This could have been my head," he said, a bloody bandage clinging to his chin. "If I ever see you riding without one again, I'll kill you myself."

I was mortified as only a teenager could be.

"Robert said I could stay here while I recuperate.

Leona and Shea went back to Tennessee with her family for a month or so."

Neither Robert nor Reba, my mom, had mentioned a houseguest. I always obeyed Robert because I was a bit afraid of him. "Sure. Can I get you anything?" I muttered trying to be helpful.

"A bed," he said then clambered through the door and hobbled behind me to our guest room.

Over the next week or so we spent every afternoon together. We ate together, watched TV, played games, mostly in the spare bedroom. On the days Reba was home from her hairdressing job, she tried but could not keep me out of there. I was fascinated and he was flirty. He was full of Percodan and other glorious painkillers most of the time, which made him fun and funny. Although at the time we never confessed it, both of us knew that feelings were emerging.

School had been released for the summer for less than a month when Cookie was well enough to go home. For the first few days, the teenage gang was a bit tentative as they gathered around him to listen to stories of motorcycle racing, Evel Knievel and parties. He had raced professionally and knew all the top riders from the tour like: #9 Gary Nixon from Cockeysville, MD; #10 Dave Aldana, from Santa Ana, CA; #38 Chuck Palmgren from Santa Ana, CA; and, #1 Jay Springsteen, from Lapeer, MI; all of whom are now in the American Motorcycle Association Hall of Fame.

I enjoyed the stories he told and had no idea that someday I too would party with this hardscrabble bunch. He had traveled all over the U.S. and most of us in Easton had never been out of the state. I learned he had been forced to join the Marine Corps right out of high school for some behavioral infraction involving bonfires in the streets. This did not deter me. I longed to travel with him, someday, somewhere, because of our infatuation and because I really wanted to get off the Eastern Shore.

Soon, he was back to playing hand games to see whose reaction times were fastest. I think it may have been an excuse for us to touch. My friends began accusing him of playing favorites. They knew he liked me best. I knew, too.

One day, after the other kids had gone home, I coyly followed him into his study. I wanted to see what the inside of the house looked like. He worked on the road Monday through Friday selling motorcycle parts to dealers in the Mid-Atlantic and all the orders and expense reports lived in his den. The room was piled with reams of papers simply dumped against the wall.

"What on earth happened in here?" I asked.

"Paperwork. I hate it. I don't mind selling, but I can't stand the filing and reports," he answered. "Hey, you're a smarty pants. Want a job?"

"Really?" I said, barely able to contain my excitement. "With pay and everything?"

"Of course I'll pay you. But you have to fill out my expense reports, file them through the mail and organize all these files into that cabinet. Then, as I get home each week, keep the system going," he explained. "Beats babysitting."

"Are you kidding? By miles," I added. Gazing at the multiple stacks of papers and folders against the walls, more timidly I prodded, "So, how much will you pay me exactly?"

I drove a hard bargain but we settled on fifteen dollars a week. And, the best part was I got to spend time at his house – often with him.

While sitting amongst the reams of papers, we talked, joked, laughed and learned more about each other. I exaggerated to make him think I was more mature than I actually was, including embellishing details of my previous boyfriend encounters. At mid-week when he was on the road, I would raid the sherry in his liquor cabinet. I began to feel so comfortable there; it was like having my own house. The thought of Leona returning didn't enter my mind. When he arrived home on Friday, he had been drinking. Once I finished up the work and prepared to leave, Cookie turned on the sales charm to convince me to come back later that night. I said I'd try. My fear was not nearly as great as my anticipation.

My friend Nicki, Cookie's next-door neighbor with long black hair like Cher, came to sleep over at my house. We were camped out in my basement bedroom, which actually was the only part of the basement that was truly underground. Our house was built on a sloping hill with the front appearing as a single level rancher and the back façade stood two stories tall. There was a screened porch with sliding glass doors into the piano room and one entered my bedroom from a door off that room. Next to these rooms were a laundry area, half bath and garage.

My room was well appointed in '70s chic with a built in desk, closet and plastic media cabinet all painted electric blue and lime green. The gold veining in the white paneled walls gave off a warm glow. I slept in my mother's old double bed, part of a typical mid-century modern bedroom suite my grandparents bought her just before she married my dad. My room felt safe and private, two very important characteristics for a young girl's room.

I was bursting. I couldn't wait to tell her I was going to sneak out across the street to see Cookie.

"Are you sure you know what you're doing?" asked Nicki, ever the conservative voice of reason. She didn't want me to go and didn't want to be caught in my room alone. She was a good friend and we'd been close since we wrote a song together for one of my school classes.

"Not really but he asked me to come." I said matter-of-factly. "It'll be fine. I'll be back before you know I'm gone." I tried to sound confident but nervous didn't begin to describe what I was feeling.

I left at about 11:30 p.m., after hearing Robert and Reba go to bed. Once they cranked up the window air conditioning unit, they couldn't hear thunder. Slowly sliding the glass doors open to the screened porch, I stole out, darting from bush to bush trying to hide my path from any nosy neighbors who might be peering out into the night. My knees were shaking as I ran.

Chapter 5

THE ALMOST FIRST NIGHT

WHEN I GOT to the front stoop by skirting between the shrubs and the house, he was lying there shirtless and asleep, a nearly empty bottle of Bacardi next to him. His tanned, naked torso stirred me. I was standing on the ground, putting him about chest level to me on the top landing. As I tapped him softly on the shoulder, he turned and wrapped his arm around me landing a huge, passionate, uninhibited, wet French kiss. The sweet burn of rum lapped my tongue. It reminded me of the sensation I got when just a few years earlier I delighted in the theft and consumption of juicy grapes from my grandparent's neighbor's grapevine – forbidden and addicting. My legs nearly buckled as my heart pounded harder. I had been kissed before but this was like being four shots of bourbon drunk after tasting only a single bottle of beer.

Suddenly, he was wide-awake and coherent. He grabbed my arm and dragged me inside the dark house. The screen door clanked shut and we lay down on the living room floor side by side and continued to kiss. Kissing was something at which I was practiced. As the petting got heavier, my excitement grew into apprehension.

I hesitated as he put my hand down his shorts. With his other hand, he pulled up my top and exposed my breasts. He was older and much more experienced than any boy I knew. "This is a good thing," I told myself. He knows what he's doing. He's not stupid like the teenagers who get themselves pregnant. But he was drunk and I was half undressed and slowing down perceptibly. Seeing myself naked was one thing, but seeing him naked was totally another!

Taking a deep breath to help calm my nerves, I played the loop in my head, "I was wise in choosing an older man who would teach me." But I had not had enough birthdays or boyfriends to be completely fearless. Brushing my hand over his erect penis under his cutoffs, I jolted up in a panic that would not be quelled.

He tried to coax me back to the floor, but I had reached full whirlwind mode. I was more scared as questions popped into my head: "What if Leona comes home? What if my parents notice I am gone? What if he realizes I don't know as much as I said?" I had put this event in motion but this wasn't the ideal scenario for my first encounter.

Putting myself back together, I raced from the house. My heart was flying faster than my feet.

When I landed at home with Nicki anxiously awaiting my return, I was breathless. Describing in painstaking detail as only a teenager could, I proceeded to tell her everything. She was aghast but loving every morsel. It was the biggest secret <u>ever</u>.

Chapter 6

D-Day

IN THE NEXT couple of days as I etched that night's events into my brain, a pattern emerged. This was good. I didn't want to get pregnant, so, if I was going to do it anyway, it should be with someone who knows more than I do. It was almost as if it were preordained. A teacher, delivered directly across the street – just for me. Leona was out of sight, and I had to put her out of mind.

On Monday, I went to work as usual, hoping the fear was not still plastered on my face. He greeted me as if nothing had happened. I sat on the couch and began sorting files. He joined me. "I'm sorry if I frightened you," he whispered.

"No. It's okay. I…it was just a lot all at once," I stammered.

"I would never do anything to hurt you. Or force you into anything," he said.

"I know. I do want to. But…well, I want it to feel 'right,' you know?"

"I do. Let me ask you something. Do you know how I feel about you?" his eyes, dark brown pools, locked onto mine.

"Well, I think…"

"I want you to know. I love you. I love everything about you. I would die for you," he gushed.

Wow. He said it. It was the first time a man had said these words to me in a romantic context. I, of course, loved him too. But I remained cautious.

"That's great. I love you too. But…" I hesitated, "you're married."

"Yes, right this minute I am. But I don't have to be. Why do you think she has been gone so long? Things are not happy. They haven't been for some time. You want me to be free? Done." Just like that, he said it.

"You'd leave her for me?" I asked.

That was all I needed to hear and at my age, I was not focused on the consequences. I was ready, so we made a plan. My parents were going to the drive-in movies that Saturday, July 28.

I made up an excuse to my twin brothers' babysitter that I was going to Nicki's for dinner. I pretended to go to Nicki's house, but ducked into Cookie's back door instead. He was preparing dinner. We ate steak, laughed and drank wine. Eventually he led me upstairs.

It was warm but a breeze blew softly in the windows. He was gentle and loving but as he passed our previous makeout barrier, I balked. "Should we use protection?" I asked.

He complied, and came walking back toward me, fully erect. As we awkwardly tried to get things moving, I yipped. It hurt and I started to cry. My cover was blown. He knew I was a virgin.

"Hey, hey, it's okay. Why didn't you just tell me?" he pleaded.

The floodgates already open, I poured out the whole plan. He was more experienced. I thought it was safer. I pretended to be more experienced. The more I cried, the more he made me feel better. He kissed every inch of my body and soon I was lost. No more tears to stain the pillow. Just entry into the sea of adulthood, with waves so large and storms so wicked I could never have imagined.

Chapter 7

Do I look different?

I MAY NOT have looked any different, but certainly I acted it. I knew the score. I was an adult. I could handle this being in love stuff. No sweat. That confidence was somewhat short-lived when I ran into my first adult in our kitchen. Guilt raced up and illuminated my face. Did it show? Could my mother tell?

"What are you doing today?" Reba asked.

"Nothing special. I'm going for a ride later," I said as calmly as possible, hanging my hair across my eyes.

"I thought you were out of gas," she said, referring to the Honda.

"No, my ten speed. I feel like I need some exercise," I sputtered.

"Well, watch the cars if you cross the highway," she warned in Mother-speak and went on about making food.

Okay. Relief set in when my face didn't betray me. But, the nearly impossible task of keeping our relationship secret in a tiny town lay ahead. I was to meet him at the arboretum. The bird and tree sanctuary, thick with summer leaves, was on the outskirts of town on a little-used road. There, he could hoist my bike into the back of the van and I could vanish for hours at a time. It became "our place."

It was magnificently breezy and warm as I rode toward our tryst. I could feel the anticipation swelling up in me as I pumped each pedal. I felt connected to a whole new universe, fed by surging hormones.

As I coasted closer to the sanctuary, I glimpsed the corner of his van perpendicular to the road. My heart leaped as he slid out of the driver's door. I checked over my shoulder for oncoming traffic but the road was deserted. It was safe. The birds sang gleefully as he loaded my bike in the back and we climbed in behind and closed the doors. We kissed passionately and deeply. To enhance my education, Cookie often brought a variety of magazines that photographically instructed on the various sexual arts – fellatio, cunnilingus, positions, etc. I wouldn't have exactly called it pornography, it was more like sex education and I was after all an "A" student.

Leona and Shea had returned home, so Reba had re-ignited the friendship she had struck with Leona before they left. The women planned date nights for the two couples and Cookie hated it. He wanted to be with me. My jealousy burned a hole through Leona each time I saw her. But, when Reba announced that Cookie and Leona would be coming to visit us on our yearly beach trip, I had mixed emotions. A whole weekend with a house full of others to preoccupy Leona's time and not enough beds...sounded like an opportunity to me.

The townhouse next to Silver Lake in Rehoboth, Delaware was a three bedroom with a pullout couch in the living room. The roster included Robert, Reba, me, my twin toddler brothers, our part-time nanny Miss Sadie, Robert's sister Denise, her husband, their two toddlers and a teenaged Au Pair. Add Leona, Cookie and Shea and the tiny place was overstuffed. So, Au Pair and I volunteered to sleep in the flattened back of Mom's green Oldsmobile Vista Cruiser and Cookie decided to sleep in his van. Once exhausted Au Pair nodded off, I slid out the open window and quietly changed venues to Cookie's van. I'm not sure if it was the newness of our relationship or the danger of being together right under their noses, but it was HOT! As I re-remember, it could have been humidity and summer heat minus air conditioning.

Just before sunrise, I crept out of the van and hopped on my 10-speed for an early morning ride.

This way, no one would know I hadn't slept in the back of the station wagon. I was feeling good and grown up, but as the day progressed, my adolescence reared its ugly head.

Some weeks before, I had borrowed my grandmother's engagement ring. I was making my public solo singing debut at the Cambridge Moose lodge accompanied by my Mom's second cousin's country band. I wore a tight, silk-like blouse with bright jewel tones and green wide leg pants with white platform heels and sang "I Wish I Was a Teddy Bear." To complete my look, I needed a sparkling ring on the hand that held the microphone and my grandmother had obliged. She was coming to the beach to visit for the day and I intended to return the ring then.

After lunch I donned my bikini and hit the beach. I was happy on the sand and hated going into the water. I didn't like the gunk and critters on the bottom and I was fearful of large waves. Ever the salesman, Cookie coaxed me into the surf. Before I knew it I was down under one wave, then another. The waves got larger and I was unable to resurface. As my right hand grasped at the moving sand on the bottom, I gulped seawater. I was about to drown, as Cookie's hand hooked the back of my top and he plucked me from the crashing waves. As he pulled, my soul shrieked, "Noooooooooo!" My fingers clawed the sand as I felt the precious ring slipping off my finger. I coughed up saltwater then plunged my fingers back deeper into the sand to retrieve the diamond, but the tide had claimed it.

As he hoisted my waterlogged body up the beach, my wailing filled the huge open space, punctuated by saltwater coughs. Blankets of people up and down the strip gawked at my remorse. He tried to console me by saying he'd get me another one, but my ears were not receptive. As soon as my legs would hold me, I ran right past my grandparents into the townhouse bathroom and locked the door.

I cried for hours and would not come out, nor let anyone in. I had let my grandmother down. I should not have been wearing the ring. Despite a massive search effort for the rest of daylight, it was never found. My grandparents, Cookie, and Leona left, and I didn't speak to anyone for the rest of the beach trip. I grew up quite a bit on that vacation.

Hard as it may be to believe, Cookie and I trysted often and remained undetected for weeks. I was too tired one night to slip out the sliders, so Cookie took the huge risk of coming to my room. I left the door unlatched and he sneaked in the same way I sneaked out. I had a chain lock on my bedroom door that I hooked once he was safely inside. We were lying on the bed after making love when I heard footsteps on the stairs. Reba must have heard some noise – didn't I hear the air conditioner fire up? – then come down to investigate.

Cookie was small in stature, a very helpful characteristic in this situation. He glued all five foot six of himself to the far side of the bed and squished underneath as far as possible. Luckily, it was dark in the room when Reba opened the door, only as far as the chain latch would allow.

"Are you awake?" she said.

"Yeah," I replied, the adrenaline rushing to my face. "What?"

"Are you on the phone? Do you know what time it is? And why is the door latched?" the mother speak continued.

"I was talking to Jeannie, but I'm off now and going to sleep. I had a bad dream earlier so I locked the door." I felt as if my face would explode. I was sure she could hear my heart's telltale beating.

Jeannie was my school friend who was notorious for staying up late. I had been in my room for hours so I could have fallen asleep earlier and awakened to share the dream with my girlfriend. The plausible story let us both off the hook, as Reba retreated upstairs satisfied with my explanation. The relief in the room was palpable. We were very quiet and waited a long time before attempting to extract him without incident. He never returned to my room again. Too risky.

We had one more highly memorable close call at his house one evening. Leona was out for the evening and Shea was safely tucked into bed dreaming. Right after the dusk sank into darkness, I sneaked in the back screen door and found Cookie on the loveseat in the den. The petting ramped up to a hot and heavy pace as the humidity wafted in the open windows. Suddenly he started upright.

"I heard a car," he said jumping to his feet. "Get out of here now!"

I was trapped. The back screen door was creaking open and there was no clear path to the front without being detected. I felt Cookie's hand grasp the back of my jean shorts and with one huge lunge he threw me head first out the open window to the side yard. I landed with a thud on the grass face up. I must have somersaulted but I don't remember it. I dared not move or make a sound as I lay on the cool ground and listened for voices from the house. No shouting. No arguing. When all sounded normal, I crawled away toward the neighbor's house then crept, flitting from bush to bush like a butterfly, finally making my way back to my room. Phew and ouch!

Chapter 8

———∞∞———

SWIMMING

THE THICK SUMMER air was sweet with honeysuckle and cut grass and I was feeling none the worse for wear after my defenestration. Heat and humidity were part and parcel to Augusts on the Chesapeake Bay yet that didn't stop Shelly and me from complaining about it. Shelly was the neighborhood tomboy who was my daily riding partner on the motorbike trails, now that we had outgrown the numerous ponies we both had enjoyed. She had an above-ground pool in her backyard but since her father left in the divorce there was no one to clean and fill it for the season. I guess the birds enjoyed it.

As we gazed at the blooming pool of algae wishing for the clear blue of chlorination, a loud muffler cut through the lazy, heavy afternoon. Cookie pulled up behind the back porch where we were perched. I had confided in Shelly about our relationship because I believed she really didn't care what I did and she was not the gossipy type.

Under cover of the sputtering engine, the three of us conspired to meet that night to go swimming. Shelly and I would sneak out and head to the vacant corner lot where Cookie would pick us up in the van, then proceed to his grandmother's estate and its in-ground pool. At 93, "Muddy" was half blind and half deaf so there was no threat of being discovered.

None of us had a problem stealing out. The plan was clicking along as we girls piled into the van toward a summer dip. The half hour drive served to enhance the forbidden nature of our voyage.

The estate was very dark on our arrival. Cookie got out and turned on the pool light that came on dim and slowly brightened. Cookie and I didn't care about swimsuits, but Shelly was modest. Finally after we turned away, she got in, staying in the shallow end. Cookie and I swirled in the deep end, closer to the light. As the moon shone down on us it felt like I was dreaming. The thought never crossed my mind that the bliss could and would end someday. A slight tactical error of leaving behind three wet towels should have been our downfall but somehow wasn't. Luck or fate was on our side, for that moment.

A couple of hours later, well after midnight, when

we approached Stoneybrook all the lights glaring from each of our houses telegraphed trouble. We were busted. After a moment of panic and quick coordination of the story, Shelly and I bailed out of the van and trekked back to our respective residences on foot.

Shelly's mom had awakened to check on her and found her bed empty. She started calling the neighborhood friends' parents to ask if there was a sleepover. When my mom went to check on me – I was out too. Figuring they knew we were together, we became each other's alibi. Our story was that after we sneaked out, every time we saw a car coming near, we hid. We both said we didn't realize it was someone we knew looking for us.

Cookie returned to his grandmother's house and slept outside on a pool chaise. That way, he could explain the towels. "I got real wet," he deadpanned later as he fought with Leona for not coming home. This argument was pivotal since it caused her to pack Shea in the Datsun and temporarily bunk at a friend's house in town. It didn't matter that she and my mother had caroused around town with whomever they chose without consequence. I know this because Cookie and I were bored one night and decided to follow them to the local bar and watch their shenanigans.

Shelly and I got into big trouble for sneaking out, and although my shoulder length hair was still damp in back, no one put the clues together about where we really were.

Chapter 9

———⚬⚬⚬———

To L.C.,
Love Always, Cookie

EARLY SEPTEMBER ROLLED around much too quickly and my idyllic summer days turned into deskbound fights with the Sandman. High school was great; don't get me wrong. There was a lot to be said for high school jocks in their letter jackets, dances, football games, plays and the like. Class work came easily to me, and my midriff tops didn't hurt my popularity any. The problem was I was sleep deprived.

My schedule began at 8 a.m. with classes until 3:30 p.m., then an hour and a half of flag carrier practice with the band. After dinner there was homework, followed by sleep from about 10:00 p.m. until 2:00 a.m. At two, I would throw on a sweater and a pair of jeans and soundlessly slide the glass patio door open to slip across the street to see Cookie. We attacked each other furiously to ward off sleep and just before dawn I would sprint back to the safety of my room. A nap before the school bus arrived left me about three hours short on shuteye every night. It didn't occur to me at the time that this was unusual. I had more energy than five people, most of the time.

I never was a morning person and my midnight ventures abetted my Garfield-like a.m. personality. First period Geography usually was appealing, full of films of exotic locales. One film too many put me out on my desk and summarily humiliated by Mr. Thompson, who also coached junior varsity football. By the way he tormented me, I could have sworn he knew my secret and was deliciously jealous. He was not a friend of Cookie's but by the way he looked at me, I believe he knew something was going on.

After weeks with bags under my eyes, we took a few nights off. I needed sleep to fuel my creativity. Cookie's birthday was approaching on September 28 and I had no idea what to get him. Coincidentally, he shared the same birthday with my grandmother, the other person I was closest to in the world. She and I had a strong bond and perhaps that explains some of the intense feelings I had for Cookie — the difference being that his Libra air sometimes fanned my Aries flames and the combustion could be dangerous.

We had planned an afternoon trip to Baltimore on the approaching Saturday (I told Mom I was going to Salisbury with some friends) and the answer to my gift quandary was never more clear than after that day.

We met at the bird sanctuary, securely stowed my bicycle in the back of the van, and drove northwest over the Bay Bridge. I had never been to Baltimore, so it seemed as large and metropolitan to me as New York. After a driving tour through the Lutherville industrial park where Cookie's job was headquartered, then through his childhood street, we stopped for lunch at a Japanese steakhouse where ninjas masqueraded as chefs and fully cooked food flew off a hot grill like a magic show. Doesn't everyone fondly remember the first time they visited a teppanyaki?

During the end of the Vietnam War the legal voting and drinking age had been lowered to 18 years, so I ordered a glass of wine. (It took the Republicans of my parents' generation until 1984 to discover a way to continue to allow 18 year-olds to vote but not allow them to drink. That year, Congress denied federal highway funding to states with drinking ages below 21.)

Cookie ordered a Cuba Libre, his cocktail of choice, and we celebrated our freedom from anyone who knew us. Unlike today, there was lax penalty for restaurants that served minors, and a girl with a date old enough to be her father was never carded.

At the end of a really fun meal with a couple of drinks under our belts, a small velvet box appeared on the wooden plank that had served as our table. "Go ahead," he said.

"Open it."

Scared, but too excited to care, I cracked the clamshell. A slim gold band with four diamonds channel set in the center gleamed back at me. I took it out and read the inscription, "L.C., love always, Cookie." It was our code. He always called me his love child (L.C.).

He removed the ring from my hand and pushed it on my finger. "Each diamond represents a year that I have to wait for you, and I will. But once you are legal, I want you to marry me." The ring was a portal to our future.

Any other time it was a practically impossible task to shut me up, but at this moment I was speechless. I cried a little, we kissed and I managed an "okay."

A proposal to a 14-year-old only seems amiss in our post World War II culture. Before that, when life expectancy was much shorter, it was not that unusual. Back in the van and rolling south over the Bay Bridge I regained my composure and quipped, "So, you've got four years to get your divorce." I was half kidding, but that event was to come a lot sooner than my high school graduation.

My new gold band sealed the deal on his birthday

present. I had to get him a ring, too. One of my best friend's parents owned a jewelry store in town, so after school I rode my bike there to peruse the inventory. I had a little money, but not enough for the gold and onyx initial ring that I felt was perfect.

Since they knew me, I talked them into a payment plan - $15 dollars down (a week's pay for me!), then $10 a week until the entire $49.99 price plus tax was paid in full. I left very specific instructions not to send a bill to my house. I would come in every week and pay, in person.

Everything was too perfect. He loved the ring and I had no idea how he would explain it, but it didn't seem to matter. I was hiding mine on a chain around my neck, long enough to hide the ring in my cleavage.

Then one day, as I plopped my book sack down on the couch after school, my mother, waving an envelope in the air, asked me if I had been shopping. I gulped and my mind raced to concoct a story she would believe. "Yes," I said. "I bought Doug a ring for his birthday." Doug went to my high school, we had dated once or twice and Mom had met him. In another of a series of lucky breaks where the universe covered for me, Doug's last initial was S, the same as Cookie's and the one on the ring.

"That's a lot a money to spend on some kid. How do you think you are going to pay this bill? I am not giving you the money," sniped Reba.

"I work. And besides, I told them not to send a bill. They told me I could pay $10 a week until it was paid off and I agreed to come in person and do that," I said in crescendo. "You have no right to tell me how to spend money I earned!"

I didn't know it at the time, but this credo would become a theme in my future relationships. I still do not like to be told how to spend my own money.

Moral of the story: when one of your friend's parents owns the local jewelry store, do not expect discretion – or for them to believe that a 14-year-old will honor her debts.

Chapter 10

THE PARTY

THINGS WERE VERY quiet after that. The entire winter seemed eerily still. Maybe the abundance of darkness camouflaged our passion. Even the telltale footprints I left in the nighttime snow didn't give away our secret. We cut back on our meetings a little because it was cold and being outside for long periods was not as easy.

When winter eased into spring my fifteenth birthday approached. I planned a party at my house, to be held in the basement. The typical rules applied: no beer, and no boys who were not on the approved guest list.

I agreed, knowing full well that both were long shots not to happen. Cookie wasn't happy that I would be just across the street and out of reach, drinking and having fun without him. After the obligatory inspection by Mom, the party kicked in as other boys arrived from the back lower level door with full coolers they stashed outside the porch.

I had imbibed a bit and was sitting on the lap of some guy I hardly knew. He had braces and I wondered what it would be like to kiss someone with braces. I wasn't attracted to the guy. It was sheer curiosity that led me to the lip lock. Just as I did it, I heard a commotion on the porch. Staring at me through the sliding glass was Cookie, checking up.

There was not much I could say. This wasn't the first time I had made a bad judgment call under the influence of Boone's Farm Strawberry Hill or beer. He grabbed me by the arm and yanked me into the powder room. I sat on the toilet lid as he looked down and berated me. He was not sober either and we ended up crying in each other's arms. I apologized and confessed my experiment, stressing that it didn't mean a thing.

He finally collapsed to the floor and forgave me. Just in time, too. Mom's footsteps coming down the stairs were unmistakable. We shushed each other and whispered a plan. I would flush, turn off the light then go out into the den, closing the door almost all the way so no one could see inside the windowless half bath.

This was not my lucky night. Mom smelled beer and so I was convicted again without a trial. I told her I didn't feel well so I was in the bathroom. "No wonder," she said. "Everybody out! The party's over!"

She was about to send me to my room when she got suspicious about the bathroom door. "Why did you shut the door? What are you hiding? Is there more beer in there?"

Pushing back the hollow door with her right hand and turning on the light with her left, she shrieked when she saw Cookie sitting on the floor, halfway under the sink.

Ordered to my room, I listened through the door as her tirade grew longer and louder. "What are you doing at a kids' party? How is this appropriate? If you knew they were drinking, why didn't you come up and get us? Some friend of Robert's you are!" Two sets of footsteps ascended the stairs to Robert waiting in the main floor living room.

I sneaked up and listened at the upstairs hall door. Cookie kept his cool like the salesman he was and talked his way out of this dead-to-rights situation for the next two hours. He played the "concerned neighbor/ friend" card over and over. He told Mom he caught me kissing nameless guy and knew I had been drinking, so he was scolding me in private. "I didn't want to embarrass her at the party. I was trying to diffuse the situation," I remember him saying. It was unbelievable but amazing. By the time he finished they were thanking him.

We chilled on seeing each other for the better part of two weeks, then Leona showed up for a few days to collect some of her belongings. Although she wasn't living with him, there were no official separation papers so she came and went as she pleased. It didn't take long for her to hear the gossipy aftermath of the party. Leona was not Mom. She smelled something fishy and went about methodically baiting the hook.

Chapter 11

MIDNIGHT CALLER

SOON, YEARNING WON out and I went to his house in the dusk of evening. I'm not sure where Mom and Robert were, but I was able to cross the street without detection. We made love then talked in his bedroom, calmly, quietly unaware there was a storm coming.

Two nights later the private line in my bedroom rang at midnight and I answered groggily thinking it was Cookie. "Hello."

"What the hell do you think you are doing fucking my husband?!" screamed the raging Leona.

"What are you talking about?" I mumbled.

"Don't play dumb with me you little home wrecker! We both know there's nothing dumb about you. I know what you are up to. I put a tape recorder under the bed. I know you were there and I have evidence. Just admit it and maybe - just maybe - I won't have to come over there and wake up your parents."

"What do you want me to say? You two are separated. What difference does it make to you who he sees?" I asked.

"You had better call it off and if you ever set foot in my house again, not only will I tell your mother, but I may have to kill you." Click. My adrenaline surged as if I had run a sprint.

Ring. "Were you talking to Leona? I hope you denied everything! She's crazy and there is no way she has a tape," Cookie spat.

"I didn't say much. I didn't really admit or deny it. She was too busy screaming; said if I admitted it, she wouldn't tell Mom," I told him.

"I don't care what she said. Don't trust her. Deny, deny, deny, no matter who says what. She's bluffing about the tape. Somebody was spying and told her they saw you. Don't ever admit it," he insisted. "Love you. Gotta go." Sleep was not my friend that night. I tossed and turned every possible scenario over in my mind. A sense of doom permanently attached itself to my demeanor.

A couple of days passed and I was beginning to think Leona had kept her word. Wearing the newly sewn, jersey-knit turquoise maxi dress I made in Home

Ec and the trusty white patent leather platform shoes, I strolled down the street from Marcia's house after church. Mandatory church was our penance for her hippy trysts.

Both Robert and Mom were waiting in the kitchen for me. My white Trimline princess phone was laying on the counter strangled by its own cords, ripped from the wall: a symbolic but effective gesture; taking away my line of communication when they weren't even paying for it.

I felt sick. My world was about to crumble before my eyes. Leona had indeed shared her suspicions with Reba and Robert, although he didn't say much. Mom did all the talking and he was just there as the enforcer.

Needless to say I was grounded for life, but as instructed I continued to deny everything. "I am not crazy but Leona is. She is bitter and jealous of all of us because we still have a good life and she doesn't," I told Mom. My persuasive skills were underdeveloped and no one believed my denial. The party incident didn't help my case. This was a tragic blow but I was determined that it was not over. Phone or no phone we would find some way to avoid detection and hook up, like salmon that needed to spawn.

Chapter 12

———— ⁓⁓ ————

GREEN EYED MONSTER

I WASN'T CONVINCED our Shakespearean romance was devolving to its inevitable tragic end, I just knew our times together were far fewer and more clouded with external complications. Penned into my half acre yard and transported to school only by official bus or parental car, I was miserable in teenage prison.

Cookie took it in stride, continuing to drink and flirt with other women, his adult freedom uncurtailed. We were taking a break for the heat to cool down, plus communicating was a big challenge. On the bright side, he spread the word that his divorce paperwork was moving along.

My school friends took pity on my plight, although

they didn't know the complete reason for my punishment. The party officially was to blame, but the details of my neighbor and me rounded town in whispers and speculation. Not that any of the girls in my school had any room to talk, as more than one of them had spent time at the free clinic to "take care of" a pregnancy. One even asked me to accompany her since the male responsible acted more than a bit reluctant.

Another friend took pity on my incarceration and introduced me to a senior on the wrestling team. Richie was a six feet, two inch blonde with Adonis' body. He wasn't the love of my life, but soon the sex was a nice distraction. Because he was close to my age and Mom knew his mother, she eased up on my restrictions a little at a time. By then, I had mastered the art of the small, cover-my-whereabouts lie.

Richie and I went to several dances and cruised the bowling alley in his light blue Ford Cougar while swigging from a bottle of Tango. When bravery overtook intellect, we cut school and spent the day at an abandoned farmhouse, drinking, sunbathing on the roof in the nude and making good use of the old mattress left behind in the upstairs bedroom.

We grew rather close, but his immaturity was always a barrier. He nearly got me into more trouble one rare night while I was at home babysitting, another perk of my punishment. Robert had fixed up a cobalt blue Chevy Camaro SS350 with white racing stripes and intended it for me when I got a driver's license. Richie came calling, begging to borrow the Camaro for a street race on the back road near the dump. He had disabled the Cougar the previous Friday night by landing it in a ditch near the Catholic School.

It was stupid of me to give in and I sternly demanded that he be back by 10:30 p.m., well before my parents usually returned home. Pacing for nearly two hours, I worried he had wrecked my car. By 10:57 p.m., the blood in my face boiled with anger. Tick, tock. I would be in double trouble in less than half an hour.

Finally at just a click past 11, Richie came roaring into the driveway, machine intact, meeting me at the garage door to stow the car. I turned on the floor fan in the garage and opened the car hood to cool the engine. Richie high-tailed it out of the house and my parents arrived just 10 short minutes later. Relieved that Robert was too bushed to putter around in the garage, I withdrew to my room. Maybe I was addicted to the danger of being caught, but this kind of risk fed into the void where Cookie's affections had been.

In spite of Cookie's own indiscretions, my dalliance with Richie burned into him like a hot muffler. When we had a moment to talk, he berated me for practicing my newly acquired carnal skills with someone else. Once, when Richie was at my house, I thought sure Cookie was on his way over too. Just as I looked out the window, he made a U-turn and retreated. It wasn't that I didn't reciprocate the jealousy, it was my practicality that told me we needed the gossip mill to slow its grinding wheels before we could risk resuming our trysts.

For a young person without today's technology, my network of information flow was well developed. I used my favorite source, Maria, our part-time housekeeper, to glean my most valuable intelligence: where, for example, to procure birth control pills without parental consent, and whom Cookie had nuzzled at the local bar that weekend.

Although I had no right, I was hurt and angry that Cookie had spent the night with one of my Mom's best friends. We both knew that no immediate future was possible for our relationship and hoped that love would see us through the years to come. After a small ceremony to burn the few photos I had of him, I felt unburdened. We could get through this.

It didn't occur to me then, but this was actually the start of a pattern in my love life – bouncing between two men. Still addicted to the risk of getting caught, I repeated this pattern several times in my life, not learning the real lesson until I was well into my thirties.

Chapter 13

FIELD TRIP TO ANNAPOLIS

DURING MY TIME with Richie, the local gossipmongers reportedly ran Cookie out of town on a rail as an alternative to police prosecution. They left out the part where my Mom threatened him with death by shotgun if he ever came near me again. She also talked of pressing charges, but I refused to testify and threatened to run away if anyone involved the police. Mom knew me well enough to take my threat seriously.

The resulting truth was, Leona got the house in the divorce and Cookie got a new job in northern Virginia. We had managed to see each other once or twice in stolen moments before he moved but the distance soon took its toll.

The full impact of our separation didn't sink in until I called his apartment from a pay phone and someone named Katy answered. She said she knew all about me and would give Cookie my message. I was coming to Annapolis for a chaperoned student government field trip and would be staying at the Holiday Inn in Parole. Reba felt I was safe enough in a group with an adult. I gave Katy the date and hoped for the best.

When the bus rolled into the parking lot and I saw the psychedelic van parked in the corner, my whole body tingled with excitement. It had been months since we had seen each other. I confirmed to myself that Katy didn't mean so much to him and was pleased she did as she said she would.

I raced to check in, landing the luckiest room in the motel for sneaking out - all the way at the end on the ground floor – the room dark novels refer to as "murder central." I quickly slipped into my lowest, tightest jeans and a popcorn stretchy bodysuit, making my exit unnoticed. The geeks I was bunking with were only interested in liquor and they seemed oblivious that I disappeared for hours.

Cookie and I had a wet discussion in the van that lasted for an hour or so. The tears dampened both our faces as we confessed our love in spite of the circumstances that tore us asunder. I admonished him for Katy. He said she meant nothing to him and he would drop her in a heartbeat if I would come away with him.

Richie and I had parted ways and my long-term plan was to be with Cookie. My heart wanted to go with him that night, but my head needed to finish high school. I didn't want to be on the run from my parents and the law. I wanted a real life someday.

Again, he promised to wait for me and we sealed our agreement physically. It was about 11 p.m. when he left to drive home to Virginia but he called my room at 1 a.m. to talk some more. I had imbibed quite a bit during his drive home and I was passing out on the phone. Most of the rest of the trip was a blur but I distinctly recall a threat from the chaperone to send all of us home if anyone went missing or was caught drinking again.

Chapter 14

———— 〰 ————

THE PHONE CALL INVITATION

EVERYTHING THAT HAD happened put a strain on my mother's already tenuous marriage. Twin toddlers and a lack of spousal trust would be enough to challenge even a strong union, but throw in a precocious teenager, add a splash of friends with bad influence, and it is a formula for divorce. Mom and I moved out of Stoneybrook and into a duplex in town while the twins shuttled back and forth to Robert's on the weekends.

I didn't see Cookie at all but I wrote to him now and then. I was casually dating an older boy from the town where my grandparents lived. He was a fling, a diversion, to keep my mind and body occupied in Easton — and he helped forestall the daydreaming about another life in another city with another man.

It was spring. Field hockey season and holidays had passed and my head was filled with the fever of warmer weather and outdoor freedoms. I had enough of homework in the living room chair in front of the TV; it was time to get out of my rut.

The walk home from school was chilly, punctuated by daffodils and peeks of sunshine. I was thinking about gifts for my upcoming sixteenth birthday, the week before Easter. Plunking my heavy book bag down on the table I scanned the kitchen for a snack. Mom had late clients at the beauty salon on Fridays. The phone on the wall rang and as I answered I hopped up on the counter. "Hello…" long pause. "Hello? Is this a prank call?"

"No baby. It's me. I just wanted to be sure it was you," Cookie cooed. To this day my mom and I sound exactly alike on the phone, so caution was a good thing.

"You're taking a big risk calling me here. Is something wrong?"

"Yes and no. I got a new job. (long pause) In California. I'm calling to ask you to come with me," he said, the words oozing from his lips.

I couldn't believe it! God was taunting me. All my short life I had wanted to go to California; become an actress. If my mind had been a personal computer, it would have been racing faster than a search engine to grasp the pertinent facts, issues and decisions to be made.

Interestingly, there was a significant fact that Cookie left out of his invitation. I found out many years after when it was far too late to be useful. Cookie's uncle, his mother's brother, was Harry Ackerman. Harry was a TV producer at Screen Gems in Hollywood. You may have seen some of his many hit shows in reruns – Bewitched, Hazel, Dennis the Menace, Gidget, I Dream of Jeannie, The Flying Nun and the Partridge Family. He was married to actress Elinor Donahue, best known as Betty on Father Knows Best. If I had gone to California with Cookie, would my life be different today?

After the where, how and when questions were out of the way, we got to the crux of the matter.

"You can go to school for free in California if you are a resident. I want you to go to college," he said.

"I know, but I do have to finish high school first. If I run away, especially with you, they won't rest until they find me. We'll have every police station in the country looking for us," I reasoned.

"You'll be sixteen next week. You can quit school," he argued.

"I know, but I don't want to. School is only part of the issue. I don't want to live like a fugitive," I explained. I couldn't believe I was being this responsible.

My mind was being logical and mature but my heart was breaking. I wanted to go more than I had wanted anything, even my first pony. I just couldn't make it work in my head. It wasn't clear at the time but this may have been the pivotal moment – that one decision that each of us makes - that changed the course of my life. I believe that everyone has one of these seminal moments or crucial decisions in their life. We all may not be able to pinpoint it, but it is there. And for some people, there is more than one of these critical intersections in life's roadmap.

This was truly the end of my puerile escapades. If my heart had ruled my head, I may have had the chance to be an actress at the expense of my family ties. Being rational eventually led me to a good career in Baltimore, graduate school and writing. Following my passion then might have led to fame and fortune, or drugs and disappointment.

As we let the opportunity die, we weren't about to give up. We made another plan.

"Spring break your senior year, you'll be eighteen. You can do what you want. I will send you a plane ticket. You can come; see for yourself. If you're happy, you can be with me, go to school – whatever you want," he promised.

Two years sounded like forever to me then.

Chapter 15

A New Love

I ACED MY driving test, deftly parking Reba's Vista Cruiser between the cones. Freedom to drive did nothing to shorten the long summer before my junior year. I dallied with a few young suitors but allowed myself nothing serious. Tucked away in the back of my mind was the certainty that I would be leaving after graduation and starting a new life in California. Why waste precious emotional energy on guys with whom I would not likely have a future?

Reba came home from the beauty shop one day and announced that she and Robert were going to try reconciliation. I was not a bit happy about this. Robert was a creep for reasons I have deliberately left out. I was not going back to live under his roof. I needed a Plan B.

Plan B this time was an escape to my grandparents' house in Cambridge. The Cape Cod style bungalow built in the 1920s had been their home since 1968. The modest two bedroom on Peachblossom Avenue had been my safe house for years.

I had my license but as yet had not been able to secure four-wheeled transportation of my own. For the short term, I made a deal for using my grandfather's light blue Chevy pickup. My summer plan was to sell my motorcycle, add some work money and buy the cute yellow Opel for sale at the local Shell station. I was still working on how to pay for inspection, tags and insurance.

I got a summer job, courtesy of my friend and current employee Becky, at the local Ames department store. The hours were good and I was selected to work exclusively in the shoe department. I'm sure this position served to fuel my shoe obsession…my collection now numbers over 250 pairs. Sure, they weren't exactly Jimmy Choos, but none of my acquaintances on the Eastern Shore had ever heard of shoe designers in those days.

Becky and I took turns driving to work when we drew the same shift. Meanwhile I was methodically enacting my "buy an Opel" plan.

Pop's truck came in very handy for cruising around

the local hangouts, despite its three-on-the-column stick shift that occasionally stuck in neutral. On a typically sticky evening, Becky and I were to meet at Pizza Hut at 7:30. Swerving into a parking space, I shouted to Becky in her aqua '64 Chevy Impala. Circling the parking lot was a souped-up, dark green '72 Chevelle SS with shiny chrome bumpers and white racing stripes. As it belched the low-pitched grumbles of a Turbo-jet V-8, Becky and I checked out the two cute guys cruising us. We learned that they were both eighteen and graduated seniors from the north county high school, so we invited them to join us for dinner.

After pizza and a couple of pitchers, we girls piled in the green Chevelle and off we went to see who else was out. The action on the street was slowing to nil so we headed to Becky's house. The guys crashed in the living room and we went to the kitchen to raid the fridge of her Dad's beers.

"Which one do you want?" Becky whispered. I was somewhat shocked but happy that she would ask. Becky normally was not that considerate. "I like Mark. He's quieter," I answered. "Good, because I like Frank," she said. It was settled and without a hassle.

We went back into the living room to find them watching television. Frank found this boring and soon he and Becky were dancing. I sat down on the floor next to the sofa where Mark was lounging. Although the lighting was dim, his green eyes pierced through the long brown hair sprawled out under his quirky hat and he smiled, revealing very straight white teeth in stark contrast to his thick dark mustache. He was cute under all that shyness and hair. He leaned down from the couch and kissed me. Like one of those corny female product commercials on TV, time seemed to move in slow motion. Shortly into the deep kiss, my eyes welled up and I felt like I was melting. This was not the emotion of too many beers. This was something else. It touched my soul.

After that night we were practically inseparable. Mark worked hard during the day as a carpenter but was never too tired to drive forty minutes to see me in the evening. We stayed out late every night driving, talking, kissing and growing close. Soon, an opportunity to steal away to the beach was too perfect to pass up. Before that, I had to tell him the truth.

As the Chevelle idled in front of my grandmother's porch just before midnight, my courage emerged.

"I have to tell you about it."

"You don't have to. I told you, I don't care about your past," he said sincerely.

"You need to understand that he's coming back for me. When I graduate, he expects me to be with him and you know how important it is for me to get out of here. I can't live here. There is nothing for me to do," I rambled. The harder I tried to make him see, the more love I felt washing over me. He truly didn't care. I wondered why: maybe he didn't believe me; maybe he didn't think I would actually leave.

The next evening we left for an adventure. Mom thought I was going to field hockey camp in Pennsylvania for two weeks. The camp was only one week with the other to be spent at the beach with Mark. We couldn't get into Mark's grandmother's beach cottage until Monday, so we found a motel in Bethany for the weekend. Unlike many of his peers Mark had money, but his nerves started to show when we got to the room.

"Is this okay?" he asked.

"It's great. I can hang at the pool or the beach during the day while you're at work." After a long pause I added, "Why are you so nervous?"

We sat down on the bed. "I don't want you to be disappointed."

"I am sure I won't be. Why didn't you tell me this was your first time?"

He just smiled and I was not disappointed.

Chapter 16

BETRAYAL WITH BECKY

THE "BUY AN Opel" plan was humming along as I had sold my Honda SL70 for $125. The price tag on the square yellow box with wheels was $600, so I made up the rest with savings and work pay. I didn't communicate often with my Dad but now that I was living in the same town, it was easier to track him down. He finally agreed to pay for the new muffler the car needed to pass inspection, however it was a more difficult negotiation since the last thing he paid for was the Trimline phone that was unceremoniously torn from my wall.

My grandfather already had volunteered to pay for my insurance by adding me to his policy, so getting him to throw in the tag fee was easy. He was happy for me to give up his truck even though his health no longer allowed him to drive it. I finally had a car of my own. (What I didn't know and came to learn is that the car didn't start in the rain and the doors froze shut in very cold weather.)

Mark and I were spending all our free time together, which was helping to repair my damaged reputation in Easton. He was just two years older, had a good job and turned out to be a distant relative of my grandfather. He was quiet, nice and about the opposite of Cookie. This stability helped douse the embers left in the Stoneybrook rumor mill.

We went to dances at my school, to the beach and out to dinner. We hung out at parties with his friends. My friends didn't pay much attention because he was from another county and that made it hard for them to judge him. They knew I was content, yet secretly wondered what happened to Cookie. No one ever asked me point blank about the scandal, and I didn't volunteer info, so the story seed shriveled slowly on the grapevine.

After Cookie moved away, Leona stopped harassing me because she became obsessed with the local undertaker. The affair became a non-issue once she and Cookie finally, officially divorced and I put some distance between myself and Stoneybrook.

My grandfather had been very sick with heart trouble and pneumonia creating unusual stress in my grandparents' home. I knew he was not well but the gravity of his illness didn't fully register in my 16-year-old brain. The day before he died in June, I bounded down the steps on my way out to work and was stopped by his weak voice. He was sitting in his spot on the couch from which he rarely stirred, looking pale and weak. He asked me to shave his face.

Words on the page are completely inadequate in describing how much I loved my grandfather. He spoiled me rotten and would have given up every single possession just to see me happy.

When I was smaller, I spent more time with him than anyone else. We drove for hours, with me standing next to him on the bench seat of the pickup, talking and looking at horses. We visited his friends and relatives. He taught me every back road in four counties. We shared cherry sodas and warm peeled turnips, pulled directly from the earth of his tended garden. We ate pickled pigs feet and hot cherry peppers from the jars; we were the only family members who liked spicy food. Some days the menu included raw spring onions dipped in salt and a side of potted meat or Vienna sausages. He spoke to me as if I understood everything in the adult world. The only time we ever quarreled was when I would find his stash of whiskey behind the pickup's driver seat and empty it into the sink. I didn't like it when he drank.

I wanted to help him shave but I had never shaved

anyone else's body part. I barely survived shaving my own legs and armpits without bloodshed. I told him he would have to wait for my grandmother to come home, then off I went. Before the week was over, I would regret leaving that day.

I was awakened early the next morning by Pop's moaning from the next bedroom. He was calling my grandmother. Groggily, I got up and leaned over the railing shouting for my grandmother, "Pop's calling you!"

She came hustling up the stairs and within minutes she was wailing, "He's gone, O Lord, he's gone..."

I dialed zero (yes, zero) and ordered up an ambulance. I threw on the clothes I wore the previous day and went into the bedroom where Pop lay dying. I sent my grandmother to her room to finish dressing and I gingerly tried to perform CPR. He was gasping for air and unconscious, still I kept talking to him. The paramedics arrived, bounded up the steps and immediately picked him up to check his breathing. One burly medic hoisted Pop's frail frame over his shoulder and ferried him out to the waiting gurney. I collected my grandmother and we followed them to the hospital. I called Reba from the hospital pay phone and we waited.

Once the doctor appeared to pronounce his death, I spattered him with questions. What had been done? Was there anything else they could try? How long had they worked?

I was grasping at anything to ameliorate the pain.

It wasn't until well after the funeral that I learned the Cambridge hospital did not own a defibrillator, a device that could have made a life or death difference for Pop. This was one more in a long list of facts that confirmed my need to get off the Eastern Shore and live in a more opportune locale.

A few weeks after the funeral, my routine with Mark was nearly back to normal. I was still working at the Ames shoe department but Becky had secured a better gig at the local electronics manufacturing plant. The compensation was higher but the shifts were longer and irregular. It was well past midnight when Mark dropped me at the Peachblossom front porch. As I quietly stole inside, a note dropped from the screen door.

Shoals #134
228-0048

My grandmother was a light sleeper since Pop had passed, so I called upstairs to tell her I was home, then made a beeline to the kitchen phone. I hadn't thought about Cookie lately, perhaps because of my grandfather's death.

The Shoals motel, a mere mile away, was as close as Cookie could get without the risk of discovery by one of my family members. He answered the phone, slightly slurring and begging me to come to him. The hamster wheels of my brain were spinning overtime to invent an explanation for going out again after midnight when I had just arrived home. His words began to cut as he spewed out contempt for Mark and our date that night. I had no idea he was coming to town; he had left me no time to plan. He rambled on, more and more inebriated. Abruptly, I told him I would come by tomorrow, hung up and dialed Becky's work.

I asked her to stop by his room on her way home to check up on him. I wanted to be sure his butts didn't burn the motel down and that he wasn't too angry with me for putting him off.

In the following light of day, Cookie's face showed no trace of hangover. It did however tell me something was wrong.

"Why are you here?" I asked.

"I had to come back to settle some business about Muddy's funeral," he flatly replied. "Why didn't you come to me last night?"

"I couldn't. My grandmother knew I was home. How could I explain going out again that late? Why didn't you tell me you were coming?"

"How? ... You should have come."

"I'm here now."

"Too late."

Within a half hour I understood what "too late" meant and why a glint of guilt hid beneath his dark brown lashes. The reality of his lack of control under

SMALL TOWN SCANDAL

the influence should have registered with me at that moment. I just didn't connect that the drinking was an ongoing and constant issue.

Was I a fool for trusting Becky? Shouldn't I be angrier with him? How could I be? I was sleeping with Mark. Cookie wanted me. He called me. Becky was convenient and he was drunk. I blamed her; she was the sober one.

How could my friend since childhood do this to me? Why?

The darkness that closes in on you when you are about to faint was closest to the sensation I felt in my head. I was past so angry I couldn't see straight – I was so angry I couldn't see at all. This would not subside. The inevitable confrontation happened the next night on our double date.

Frank and Becky and Mark and I had just set out to watch the sunset at Great Marsh. Mark sensed that there was animosity between Becky and me. He urged me to confront it; so I did. I called her out on her behavior in front of our dates and the screaming fit that followed was as ugly as it gets. Hurling accusations produced no feasible motive and the vitriol left scorch marks on the marshy ground. I can't say why Mark wasn't more disturbed by the entire incident, but he remained calm and rational. He wasn't happy that I had seen Cookie but neither was he swept into the volcano of anger that ripped Becky and me apart.

Frank was completely shocked and betrayed; soon taking the car and promising to return to pick us up once he deposited Becky at home. Mark was relieved that I had not been the one to get physical with Cookie, so we waited in silence for Frank to return, crickets and bullfrogs creating our soundtrack.

I learned a few years ago that Becky died as a result of a long illness. I regret not having spoken again to my once close friend. She married, had children, divorced and succumbed to complications of lupus. I kept tabs on her life through Reba who still sees Becky's Mom and gets a report. I have no idea why she betrayed me or why I focused all my anger at her instead of Cookie. The emotional ties between him and me seemed strained and I don't understand why we continued to follow through on our plans to be together. There was some unexplainable uniting force at work on both of us. More than that, he represented hope for my future.

Chapter 17

PRACTICAL
ARRANGEMENTS

THROUGHOUT MY SENIOR year of high school Mark and I grew closer together, taking classes at the community college. He obviously knew I had feelings for Cookie, but I guess he just didn't want to believe I could ultimately choose Cookie over him.

Having my own car was a great convenience for fitting in all the necessary activities of life. I worked half days, three days a week and went to Chesapeake College the other two. On Tuesdays and Thursdays I saw Mark for lunch at the college; he was working anytime he wasn't in class. I had high school from eight until noon, then zipped over to work/study at the local newspaper Mondays, Wednesdays and Fridays.

I began by editing the School Pages, taking over the job from my old friend Shelly, adding headlines, doing layout the old-fashioned way with hot wax and an Exacto knife.

I loved the deadline atmosphere and the smell of the ink on the presses. I filled in for anyone who needed help: circulation; advertising; layout for the weeklies. Soon, I was taking on assignments for articles and photos in the paper's other sections.

Management was pleased with my enthusiasm and aptitude, so they used me as a guinea pig. The paper was to receive its very first computer to archive the classified ads. Being the new kid, I was given the pleasure of typing in all the ads and "figuring out how to work the thing." My eleventh grade typing class, where school hunk Bobby sat behind me and drove me to distraction, actually paid off as I slogged through pages and pages of classifieds. Once the ads were input, my job became a piece of cake since all I needed to do was open the file each week, delete old ads and insert new ones. Everyone on staff was duly impressed with my new productivity, so I asked for vacation over spring break.

As winter's pods became seeds in the early spring rain, I began planting seeds of my own. A couple of girlfriends in my circle were planning a train trip to

Florida over spring break. They were my cover story as I told Reba I was going along. In reality, a round trip airline ticket had been sent to my six years older friend, Candy, whose fake I.D. I often had used. Cookie sent it, as promised, so I could come to California to visit. I was to fly into San Francisco. My last obstacle was how to get to the airport in Baltimore. Candy was working and wasn't able to drive me, but fate was about to intervene again propelling me toward Cookie once more.

Wendy, a teammate from the gymnastics squad, and I were having lunch at the Eggplant, a local restaurant/bar when her crush walked in. She had filled my ears with fantasies of this mystery man for months and I was finally getting to meet him. He joined us in our booth and introduced himself. His cute freckled face was expressive, in a cocky way, as he told us about his job with a St. Michaels construction company.

Wait a minute – was he the Bryce that Mom and her new beau had been telling me about? When it became clear he was indeed that guy, the flame of jealousy burned inside Wendy so hot I could feel the heat across the table. Sure, I liked him. He was attractive and his sex appeal was undeniable. More than that, he knew his way to the airport and he would have no opinion on where I was going or why. Later, after Wendy left in a huff, he told me he was well aware of her crush and had no interest in dating her. I was a different story.

There was no malice against Mark in my sneaking

around to see Bryce. Logically, I knew I was moving after graduation (and had told Mark this several times) and immediately, I needed a ride from a non-judgment rendering adult. Reba, whose second try with Robert fizzled quickly, was thrilled that her matchmaking skills had been rewarded. She liked Mark just fine and had nothing against him, but she saw Bryce as a better match. Mark was a good man, an intent listener, faithful lover and a kind soul. Bryce was more my Mom's type; the bold, brash, outgoing, raucous bad boy. Definitely fling fabric, not marriage material; he was perfect for my needs of the moment.

I did feel a little guilty about allowing Bryce to pursue me, even though it was mainly to set up my transportation plan. Consequently, I had lost Wendy as a friend and that hurt. I considered her my best friend senior year.

One night, Bryce and I met my Mom and her friend Donna at The Pub for dinner. The Pub looked a lot like it sounded – big bar, wooden booths and floor, narrow, darkish, and very popular. Maryland has freakish weather in March. It can be 75 degrees one day and snowing the next. On this night, the snow fell deeper than usual so I felt confident that Mark would not drive 40 minutes to see me in such weather. I told him I was having dinner with my mother — which was true.

After the predictable entrees of burgers, fries, fish and chips, Donna and Reba left us in the fourth booth with our drinks. Facing the door, I could see two tall figures pushing through the crowded bar toward us. Mark, flanked by his Icelandic friend Leith, was seething as he leaned down putting his hands on the table to confront me.

Nothing I said registered. Bryce said nothing. I had warned him this could happen and told him to stay out of it. Mark was slow to anger and only exploded when circumstances warranted but he didn't believe that Mom and Donna had just left. His fingers whitened as he clasped the underside of the wooden table in a vice grip. Glasses rattled as he shook it, threatening to flip it over on top of us. Instead, after slamming his fist, he and Leith abruptly turned and fled in unison, pushing back through the puffy coats. I made a quick excuse to Bryce and followed after them, dragging my coat behind. On the snowy sidewalk I caught up and somehow convinced Leith to take Mark's car home. Mark was crying as he got in my Opel.

As his anger and heartbreak grew he clawed at the silver necklace that held my class ring and ripped it from his neck. Before I could grab it, out the window it flew into the snow. I don't remember whether logic or love saved me from his wrath, but I just kept talking and steadfastly assuring him that Bryce was not a threat. This was completely true. He was not in my life for the long term, but I knew Mark was. The only fact I kept to myself involved the ride to the airport. I couldn't risk anyone else knowing where I was really going. I had to see for myself how well my first love had survived the years and how it would stack up to the depths of feeling I had for Mark.

Chapter 18

————≈————

THE TRIP

MY ADVENTUROUS NATURE and recent eighteenth birthday didn't prevent me from being extremely nervous about my first plane flight. Bryce dropped me off as planned and promised to pick me up on my return. Bryce was older by about five years and he knew I was trying to figure things out. He was well aware that I was juggling three men and put no pressure on me.

In contrast to today, the airport was small and hassle free. No security lines, metal detectors or dogs on patrol. Flying was still considered a luxury and few people regularly partook. Someone told me to chew gum while flying, so I folded a stick into my mouth as soon as I was seated.

Except for the altitude adjustment, the flight was quite comfortable. The seats were roomy and the stews were nice. I jabbered on to the person in the seat next to me, clawing into the armrests whenever I felt a bump. I ate what they served. I looked out the window to see just how vast our country is: mountains, rivers, flat plains patchworked with fields of newly tilled soil. Then, it all disappeared beneath a fluffy cumulus cloud cover. Soon, the frosting on the Rockies peaked through the clouds and the turbulence increased, as did my anticipation. I could not believe I was really going to California.

It was getting dark when we began our descent into the San Francisco bay area. As the aircraft left the mountains behind, I looked out onto a sea of lights. As far as one could see north and south, lights dotted the hilly landscape. Then at the shoreline, an abyss of blackness called the Pacific with no horizon visible. I had never seen a more spiritually stirring sight. I wish flying still felt that way.

Cookie met me at the gate with a huge embrace. He was relieved that I had come and he wanted to impress me. As we drove a long way up to Redding, California's high desert, I strained to see the crispy, drought-ridden landscape through the darkness. His Spanish style home was a typical 1960s rancher. Arches separated the house from the covered front patio and the living room was sunken one step. Compared to the traditional east coast bungalows, it was exotic and large with a king sized waterbed to provide fun on night one.

The searing sunshine glistened off the snow-capped peak of Mount Shasta the next morning as I lay on the bow of Cookie's jet boat, "Thumper", wearing a bikini and no sunscreen. He had invited a couple of his friends, Linda and Danny, to join us on the lake. Linda was a big girl who eerily reminded me of Leona. She also had ample bosoms, so the boys quickly nicknamed us "the Boobsy twins." She sang at a local supper club where we dined that night and after a few daiquiris I joined her on stage and we sang together. As I looked out into the crowd I could see in Cookie's face how much he still loved me. I was thinking with my heart and not my head. Flattering as the attention was, I couldn't see the doom in my long-term strategy. Faults and all, I believed this man loved me; that he would have jumped out of an airplane without a parachute if I asked.

Except for the sunburn and subsequent vinegar bath, I had a great time. I liked California and I still liked spending time with Cookie. We briefly discussed what would happen in the fall. The plan was for me to drive my new Honda Civic (the down payment was an 18th birthday present from my grandmother) halfway across the country and he would fly to some Midwestern destination, meet me and drive the remainder to the West Coast. I could start school at

Shasta College, then transfer to a state university once my residency requirement was met. He could live anywhere in his sales territory so we talked about southern California, a move I hoped would put me closer to an acting career.

Chapter 19

DECISION TIME

I RETURNED TO Maryland, a whole coconut packed in my suitcase as if to prove I had been to Florida. At graduation in June, I received an unexpected book scholarship from the local Road Runners organization and was sad that my grandfather was not around to see me matriculate.

I went back to work, back to Mark and playing with my new Irish Setter puppy, Poe.

I hoped the dog would provide companionship during the long drive west back to Cookie and California. Mark had forgiven my indiscretion with Bryce. All the paperwork for college had been settled. I was all set with my BEOG grant to attend Salisbury

State College. Only Cookie and I knew I had no intention of attending the school just an hour south of my home.

The tedium of waiting that summer came to an abrupt halt for me on August 17, 1977. I strolled into work at about 11 a.m. to find a devastating one/two punch of news.

The Associated Press wire was spitting out details of the death of the King of Rock and Roll, Elvis Presley, who was found the night before in his Graceland mansion. For my sixth birthday, Reba's best friend had given me an Elvis album, "Girl Happy," and I knew every song. For years I played it over and over and watched every one of his movies. He was as talented an actor as he was a singer, and I believe he was frustrated by not having free creative reign in all disciplines. As with many other victims of overdose and because of the cover-up surrounding his death, the dangers of prescription drug abuse took decades to be revealed. I was stunned; I felt the last shreds of my childhood died with Elvis.

The second blow came at my computer, where a note was taped to the keyboard. I opened it to see the historical equivalent of a text message:

Cookie in town
Holiday Inn, 233

My emotions still reeling from the news of Elvis,

now there was a new rollercoaster in town. I had punched in at 11:02 a.m., then punched out at 11:16. I told my supervisor I had an emergency. When I arrived at the hotel and knocked on the door I was nervous. Something had to be wrong. I was planning to leave on my cross-country drive in less than a week. What was he doing here? Did he come to drive with me?

In the small room darkened by vinyl blackout curtains I discovered that his employer, BMW motorcycles, had transferred him back to the mid-Atlantic territory. This was a crisis of mega-proportions! Panic crept up my neck and clenched my jaw. Like the Cowardly Lion, I had planned to be 3000 miles away in Oz when the truth surfaced. Instead, I was faced with the prospect of telling Reba, my grandmother, and Mark, that I was to be living with Cookie somewhere within driving distance of the Eastern Shore.

His move would not be immediate. He would go back to California, sell his house and tow his boat back to Chesapeake Bay waters. I would delay college for a semester and go with him. On our return, I would shift my grant paperwork to a college in Baltimore, Towson State. The only reason this plan sounded plausible was my family rarely left the confines of the Delmarva Peninsula, and they were extremely reluctant to cross the Bay Bridge. The dread intensified in my neck as I anticipated the announcement. I was accustomed to Reba's anger and my grandmother's disdain, but it was

Mark I feared most.

Logical explanations and arguments played in a loop in my brain while I drove over the Cambridge bridge to face my inquisitors. After two hours of interrogation with Reba and her mother in the Peachblossom kitchen, I was emotionally exhausted and physically shaking. I had little fight left in me when Reba challenged me to call Mark immediately and tell him my plans. Breaking the news on the phone was a chicken's route but it gave time for him to grasp the reality. Through his wailing I deciphered that he was coming to my grandmother's house. I begged him not to drive while he was so upset.

Our mind-fogging, bowel-exsecting harangue on the front porch lasted nearly an hour before Mark jumped into his car and threatened to wrap it around a tree. I tried to stop him, reaching into the driver's window as wheels squealed and the Chevy spun away.

August 17, 1977 was not a good day.

Chapter 20

———✺———

MARRIAGE

FRUSTRATION WITH HOW I left Mark gutted like a deer nagged at me for months. The trauma of the announcement was behind me and now I tried to focus on the happy prospect of a cross-country trip. I delighted in the distraction of new surroundings and tried to push the section of my heart that belonged to Mark aside.

First, Cookie needed to sell his home in California. We made a vacation of it, flying there, driving to all his customers to say goodbye, spending a few days in L.A. seeing Disneyland, Knotts Berry Farm, Graumann's Chinese Theater, and Santa Monica Pier. It was just as I had imagined it would be, minus the brown, crunchy, shriveled grass. We even saw a legitimate actor. James

Garner was filming "The Rockford Files" on one of the studio lots we visited. He waved.

After the house closed, we trailored his bright orange jet boat, hitched it to Cookie's silver Monte Carlo and drove. Our first stop was Lake Tahoe. The Harrah's casino and I jingled with excitement and our plans to see Ann-Margret in concert. People often have remarked that there is a resemblance between us; I just wish I had her musical talent.

Our adventure continued in Laramie, Wyoming where I saw a real cowboy get thrown through saloon doors just like on old TV westerns. Our accommodations went from glitzy Harrah's to grimy Circle S motel, but I didn't mind. I was off the Eastern Shore and on with my life. The rest of the trip was long, dotted with tumbleweeds and prairie dogs.

Back on the East Coast, we found an apartment and filled it with brand new furniture. After stalking every community newspaper for a job and having no luck, I landed a part-time job at a garden center and filed the paperwork for spring semester at Towson University, north of Baltimore.

Cookie had tired of fooling around with women who meant nothing to him and soon he started guilting me into marriage. He argued that if something happened to him, all the new furniture would go to Leona. It seemed logical to me at the time (I certainly didn't have the resources to consult a lawyer) but I knew my family was not ready for us to marry. We decided to break the news gently so we set a date in late July, the 28th, the anniversary of my lost virginity. This was for the public and the big party. Another legal ceremony took place with just the two of us several months before.

The July ceremony went on as planned and surprisingly all of my family and friends showed up. Cookie's Dad was deceased but his mother Nancy came; this was our second meeting. My birth father gave me away and Nicki and my half-sister Lisa were bridesmaids. I thought it was a great party. My maternal family members were less than thrilled and I didn't have a clue that they may have been right.

Once college began, I did the normal married life tasks and learned to cook a few dinners.

I enjoyed college and did well academically. But, as months passed I began having misgivings about the marriage. Finally, I recognized some of Cookie's previous drunken episodes as a pattern. Despite saying he was happy, Cookie drank more heavily than before and our relationship was devolving quickly.

Also, there were lots of temptations at college - cute guys, pot and parties. Everyone I met was ready to party at a moment's notice. In gymnastics class, I met a girl, Elaine, who fascinated me to no end. While casually gossiping about our gym teacher, we learned we had something in common. She was my age and dating a man 15 years her senior. As we bonded over her brother's weed at a campus spot known as "the Rock," I marveled at her beauty. She had very long, straight dark brown hair and an excellent figure. Her most striking feature was her unusual eyes that enabled the admirer to see deep into her soul.

Add these circumstances to Cookie traveling for his job and drinking himself into oblivion when he got home and the sum was not positive. I had two lives really. In one, I was a typical student smoking pot in The Glen with classmates, yet still pulling As. On the other hand, I was a wife whose husband had never grown up and whose friends also were partial to self-medication.

We lived well enough from fall into the next spring, spending Cookie's inheritance from his Dad on steak and lobster dinners and motorcycle events. My patience wore thin after every party where I had to steal his car keys or have a friend pour him into the backseat. The worst cases occurred when he wasn't drunk enough and wanted to fight with me.

Fight in point: For someone born on the Eastern Shore, I had an uncharacteristic dislike for boats. Most everyone who knew me, knew this. When the California jet boat proved too unstable for Chesapeake waters, Cookie traded it for a large cabin cruiser. I had hoped he would just sell it. It was costly. I hated it. It caused arguments with thrown Heineken bottles. Yes, full bottles and they hurt. The boat and the bottle – two nails in the coffin of our relationship.

Chapter 21

DRUGS, FORKS AND ROCK AND ROLL

As I said, Cookie's traveling job meant he wasn't home often. Turned out, that was a good thing. I spent most of my free time with Elaine, eating dinner at her house, smoking pot with her, going to movies and getting to know her better.

When Cookie announced that my March spring break would be spent at Daytona's 1979 bike week, I thought it might be best to be away from Elaine for a while. I had spent a weekend in Ocean City with her and her older man and I found myself oddly jealous. I had quickly become very close to her, considered her a dear friend, but there was something more that troubled me. I felt like I was falling in love with her.

Everyone from the local motorcycle club in Lutherville was going to Florida for fun in the sun. A large contractor in Baltimore named Taylor White was sponsoring #30 Dale Singleton's ride in the race. Dale was from Dalton, Georgia, had a mop of dark hair and spoke softly with a smile. From the outset of the trip, Cookie and I were getting along well even during the non-stop partying with the racers. I met them all and they liked me – I was young.

Things didn't get out of hand until Dale won the race. All of the Winnebagos in the infield bounced with cheering fans and friends and the celebration was unlike any I had ever experienced. This was partying at the professional level. Some of the renowned racers I mentioned earlier led the charge – Chuck Palmgren, Jay Springsteen, and Dave Aldana. People called them the "three muffsketeers," for their womanizing ways. Crowds of half naked people drank, smoked marijuana, snorted lines of cocaine, disappeared with each other's mates, made donuts with their huge two-wheeled machines, vomited, then started all over again. It was insane, yet most of them are still alive today. Unfortunately, Gary Nixon, who was retired from racing when I knew him, and Dale, one of the tamer racers, are not. Dale died in a plane crash in 1985 and Gary passed in 2011.

When the victory glee died down, Cookie wanted to show me around Florida since I had never been there. We drove down to Ft. Lauderdale where spring break swung full. My first glint of anger came at the rooftop pool where my husband tried to pimp me out to some college boy from Philadelphia. Sure, he was looking at me but I truly was not interested. I guess the professional partier in him was stuck on full blast. No matter how I tried I couldn't convince Cookie I didn't want to share myself around or have a threesome. The more I talked, the more he drank, and drank. Back in our room I changed for dinner as he passed out on the bed. There was no waking him.

At about 8 p.m. with no luck in rousing the dead drunk, I went to the lobby bar, the Button. I had some food and a couple of drinks, courtesy of Mr. Philadelphia. My vengeful spirit prodded me to consummate the deal Cookie had nearly brokered earlier in the day. I got pretty drunk and don't remember much, but I do remember flirting with a nice girl who was playing pool. Her name was Toni and she wore braces.

When we returned to Baltimore, Cookie turned on the charm, played nice and attempted to make up for his behavior. Our sparring respite was short lived. When the racing circuit came to Harrington, Delaware, the muffsketeers' antics followed us home from the race to the doorstep of our apartment. Some of their entourage spun donuts on the front common area grass while the leaders of the band were doing lines off my mirrored coffee table.

The only soberish member of the group, Chuck's brother, Denny, showed off his skills as a hypnotist. He mesmerized me and suggested that my socks were on fire. I looked down and intellectually knew they were not, yet my feet were burning hot. I had to take the socks off.

Being hypnotized was a strange sensation. When your eyes are closed, you hear and are aware of your surroundings but you cannot will yourself to open your eyes. Once Denny broke the spell, I exited this altered state of consciousness not remembering any future suggestions he may have made. Later as the action peaked, I disappeared into the party van outside with two of the ringleaders just long enough to cause Cookie heartburn. Fooling around with two guys at once is not as easy as it sounds, especially when one of them was extremely well endowed. I am not sure if I received a hypnotic suggestion for this situation or not. Regardless, I couldn't prove it.

Cookie didn't confront me that night. He would never have picked a fight with his buddies, all of whom were younger and stronger. The biker band left town as quickly as they had blown in and I decided a home cooked meal could quench my two-day hangover. It was Tuesday night and the menu was spaghetti. As I poked at the meatballs with a long meat fork, Cookie began his rant about the weekend's activities.

"I figure if I can't beat 'em, join 'em. I was just partying like everyone else. It was unusual that you were coherent enough to notice I was gone. Usually you are passed out," I rationalized, knowing full well that two wrongs were just iniquitous.

I did apologize for allowing Denny to hypnotize me and for leaving without telling him where I was going. He didn't accept my apology and proceeded to dig up the unspeakable. He accused me of being in love with Elaine.

He had encouraged our friendship since most of my high school gaggle didn't live nearby. I had been avoiding her to avoid temptation. Try as I might to deny it, I had to lie. I did love her, but the feeling was not mutual – at least not in a sexual way. Neither he nor I were angels, both having our roster of marital sins, but this possibility ate him up inside. Still drinking to nurse his hangover, Cookie escalated the screaming match. Back and forth he sniped from Elaine to the ringleaders.

His anger reached a crescendo and he grabbed me by the left arm. Instinctively defending myself, I pivoted to stab him in the arm with my fork-wielding right hand. He struck back hard with a backhand across my face and I fell backward onto the toppling kitchen chair.

Silently, I pulled myself up and walked into the bedroom. I put several piles of clothing into a suitcase, scooped up my purse and keys and walked out the door.

Chapter 22

—∾∾—

EMO HOUSE

I HAD VERY little money and nowhere to go, so back to my grandmother's I drove. I stayed at my Peachblossom safe house for a week while looking for a place to rent near school. I had found a better paying job teaching exercise at a local Nutri-Systems weight loss center so I worked five days a week, four hours a day in the afternoon. College classes were in the morning and finals were upon me. The drive back and forth from Baltimore to Cambridge was killing my study time.

I caught a lucky break on a trip with Grandma in tow to retrieve some of my belongings from the marital apartment. A house on Charles Street had a room to rent and the three other roommates had chosen me as their fourth. I liked the house for its proximity to school and work and its negligible rent.

My grandmother was horrified at the dilapidated condition of the house and its formidable guard dog, Emo. He was a St. Bernard who belonged to the lead renter and his hair was literally everywhere including inside the refrigerator. As a guard dog, he excelled. He was huge, ferocious and aggressive to anyone he didn't know. Early on, that included me. I was an animal lover and he grew to accept me, so I felt safe in the house from everything except the winter weather. The house, we discovered after hundreds in oil bills, had no insulation.

I make it sound like my bounce-back was easy. The no-brainer part was leaving a man who hit me. The survival on my own part was harder, but I was determined.

I took my Geography final in the morning and had asked for the afternoon off work to collect my meager possessions from Cookie. I knew he wouldn't hit me in front of my grandmother. When we arrived at the apartment, he wasn't home. I tried to use my key but he had apparently changed the locks. This was only a minor inconvenience. I had a tool kit in my car, so I swung the hammer and broke out a ground floor window in back. I scooted through the frame, careful to push the glass aside. I was packing my things in a box and my grandmother was waiting in the car when the police arrived. A neighbor had seen me break in.

The officer asked for my identification after I explained that my name was on the lease and I was the wife who lived here. I whined that my husband had locked me out and I had no clothes to wear. In contrast to today where police are drunk with their own power and no domestic infraction is overlooked, he instructed me to take only what was mine and agree to repair the broken window. I consented.

What the officer didn't know is that I already had placed all of Cookie's grandmother's silver collection in the bottom of my box of clothes and I had no intention of paying for the window. Cookie made the repair without complaint and a week later appeared on the front lawn of my new rental with my self-propelled Hoover upright. This vacuum had been a gift to help me clean the apartment faster. He used it as a peace offering and begged me to come home. If it hadn't been so hilarious – him standing on my lawn with a vacuum pleading to my upstairs window for my return – it would have been pathetic. I had already hocked his silver collection and rekindled some of the smoldering embers of my previous relationship with Mark.

Chapter 23

TRYING TO
REPAIR THE PAST

COOKIE CONTINUED HIS stunts to get my attention and was relentless in his pursuit of repairing our marriage. I caught him following me home from work one day so I pulled over to put a stop to the craziness. I walked over to his car and leaned in the window. "I want a divorce," I said sternly.

After a diatribe of protest, he pulled his lowest punch. "If you want a divorce, you pay for it." This was his last word on the subject but I could see that he was dejected. He also felt sure I didn't have the money to pay for it. He had not yet noticed that Muddy's silver was missing. Nor did he know I had made a tidy $950 on it.

Shortly after this conversation I learned through my lawyer that Cookie had lost his job. At the time I thought it might be a ploy to avoid paying me any money. But, he moved to a smaller, less expensive apartment and began drinking even more heavily. And, still I persisted in divorce proceedings, using the silver money.

One day after work, the phone at the Emo house jangled. Emo and I were home alone. I answered as he bellowed. It was Greater Baltimore Medical Center. Cookie was in the intensive care unit suffering from pancreatitis. I felt partially responsible for his depressed mental state and the drinking that followed, so I went to visit him in the hospital.

"I knew you'd come," he said snaggle-smiling. Cookie's teeth were never in great shape. They were large and gap-ridden and he had a bridge. A Halloween costume could have used him as a prototype. He looked deathly.

"I hope this serves as a warning to you about the drinking. And, you should get your teeth fixed," I said, trying to be short and cold and not at all empathetic.

"Thanks for your concern. I nearly died," he insisted.

"I'm glad you are alive but I'm still divorcing you," I said flatly.

"You drove me to this. I can't live without you," he cajoled.

"Well, you'd better learn. I am not coming back. Mark and I are back together and you need help. You're an alcoholic." My last words hung in silence.

I knew there would be no chance of a financial settlement due to his current state of health and unemployment, and I wasn't out to make money. I simply wanted out of the marriage and I wanted what was mine. This included a stereo system that I was given as a birthday present still in Cookie's apartment. I hadn't been to his new place and I was curious. I knew he wasn't coming home from the hospital for at least a week.

The next Saturday I decided to use my precious gas ration to drive to Cockeysville to his apartment. There would be no breaking in this time and it was improbable the door was unlocked. I wasn't sure what was pushing me to go, I just had a strong feeling I should. It was a very "Trust the Force" intuition that drove me.

I walked up the steps to his door. I tried the key to our old apartment; it wouldn't even fit in the slot. I tried my mom's house key. No dice. I tried the key to the weight loss center where I worked. It fit but would not turn.

The last key on my key ring was the front door key to my grandmother's 1920s bungalow: the woman with whom Cookie shared a birthday. This is the same key I had used to open her Peachblossom front door since she moved into the house in 1968. Slowly I put the key into the slot and turned it.

I swear the door just opened as if Cookie had given me his own key. I could not believe it. Nobody would believe it! Of all the keys for all the doors in the world these two random locations worked together. Once you've had this kind of unexplainable coincidence happen to you, you always trust your intuition, even if you call it The Force.

I was aghast as I wandered into the tiny one bedroom space. It was jammed with most of the furniture from our old two-bedroom apartment. There was hardly room to step. The stereo sat on the floor next to the speakers. I unplugged the receiver and the tuner, trying to stack them and lift them together. Deciding that each piece was too heavy and delicate to chance dropping down the steps, I took them down one at a time to my car. On the last trip, I was saddened by the cramped, dark, stuffed quarters that reflected the ill state of Cookie's mind and body. As I relocked the door my sadness lifted while musing on how perplexed he would be on the disappearance of the stereo.

I did get my divorce and most of my family needed no explanation; in fact, Reba was elated. I was obligated to tell my birth father who had walked me down the aisle. He was working in the Gulf of Mexico on a supply ship for an oil-rig. We had been writing letters about twice a month since he left. Putting pen to paper is an intimate form of contact, unlike the barrage of tweets, texts and emails that fly around the airwaves now. Our inked conversations meant something as we attempted to redraw the genetic lineage that connected us. Dad had been the only adult who didn't object to my marriage and it actually seemed to bring us closer together. We came to know each other in a way not practical when I was living in close proximity to him.

My father came home to visit once during his Louisiana adventure. Meeting up with him in Cambridge filled my soul with a positive male presence I had not felt since my grandfather died. We spent most of his visit together eating, drinking, dancing, walking along the shore, talking. Some say I married Cookie to replace that older male archetype in my life and perhaps in the early stages of attraction it could have been true. Needless to say, that male model melted the longer I knew him.

I loved catching up on the years with my Dad. Because he was very intelligent yet lacking in higher education, schooling was important to him. He said no one can take an education from you and he demanded I finish college. His high school grades were good but college eluded him because of a lack of family funds, low expectations and an adventurous wanderlust that blurred his focus. He loved learning but was easily bored, quickly moving on to the next challenge. He mastered a few physical skills such as archery, fishing, baseball, cooking and carpentry. He was a sponge for book knowledge, but there were far too few practical applications for earning a living in his rural area. His second marriage in disarray, he seized the moment to explore the Gulf Coast in a job with responsibilities far below his capabilities, which left him ample time to investigate the offerings of his new surroundings.

My last letter to Dad pronounced great news; I had made the Dean's List. His last letter to me hinted that some underhanded dealings might have occurred on ship. He was vague about the exact transactions but alluded to some illegal gun trade. He did not approve.

I was young and my life was finally happy so I didn't worry. As I answered the phone on a crisp March morning, I regretted it.

Reba was crying, telling me between the sobs that my Dad had died. Killed in an accident on the ship. My hands clutched the receiver like arthritic claws, frozen in place. How could this be? He was only 39 years old and we were just beginning our relationship! What happened? How? Reba was detail-less.

I sobbed as I hung up the phone and my "house mother" roommate climbed the stairs to hug me. She prayed with me and comforted me until my body composed itself.

More sketchy tales of his accident came out at the

funeral but I still was not satisfied with what I knew. He drowned. Not likely for a former athlete. I made a pact with my two half siblings to find out anything more I could. With no money to hire an investigator, I waited. I knew I would somehow get more information.

His funeral momentarily brought me closer to my half sister and half brother, who had a far more difficult adjustment. Dad was the sun that rose and set in that boy's eyes. He went through a destructive decade, pulling up out of the muck as time healed his wounds. After a handful of more productive years, back down the rabbit hole he slid courtesy of his drug of choice. I attempted to see him a couple of times but failed. I hear through the grapevine now, although we are not in touch, that he is doing well and has been clean for a few years. For that I am grateful, and hopeful.

My half sister had only about a decade to grieve our Dad's death. When we were teenagers, she looked like me but heavier. Later, she developed Crohn's disease, had a failed marriage and could not seem to get her footing. Treatments for autoimmune disorders were sorely lacking in the 1980s – 90s and too soon she succumbed to a lung infection, a complication of her Crohn's. She was only 36. I wish I could have had more time to get to know her better.

There was no need to urge me to continue my schooling. I loved it and I did well, although I wish I had challenged myself more. A little less partying and a few more difficult classes would have served me better in the long term. For example:

I had been through a lot with the deaths and divorces and although I was cautiously settling back in with Mark, I still had wounds that I tried to assuage with drugs. Mark hated that I still smoked pot and he pretty much ordered me to quit. Never liking being told what to do, I took that as a challenge to do something stupid.

This girl I worked with at the big blue cube in Towson, a modern mirrored building that housed most of an insurance giant's staff, offered me a football. I had no idea what it was but she said it helped her work faster and have more energy. Ok, that sounded good. Luckily I took only half of it. Within seconds I felt like I could run a three-minute mile. The palpitations were so intense, I considered going to the hospital. After a little food, the speeding decelerated and I could function. I did not like speed; I was speedy enough without any help.

Later that evening I drove to the Shore to see Mark. We went out and had a few beers, which I hoped would further calm my hyped up nervous system. Unfortunately, at 3 a.m., I was still wide-awake with no prospect of sleep. In the next really stupid move of my life, I decided that taking a Demoral would help me sleep. I had purloined this script from my grandfather's medicine stash. It was great to take a half one then spend the evening at the roller rink – fearless to experiment and oblivious to the fall. Not so great on top of speed however. I completely lost my hearing and my eyes could see only black as I lay on the bathroom floor calling for Mark. I was terrified. Why he didn't call an ambulance is beyond me; and why I am still alive I have no idea. Because I did eventually regain the two senses I lost, and fell asleep to actually awake again, I made myself a promise: I was done. No more drugs.

I suppose I eventually made up for the partying by earning a master's degree – another first ever in my family. This extended schooling was made possible by my second employer, a bank that provided tuition reimbursement. I count myself very lucky, especially when I see how much student debt Millennials have today. Dad would have been proud.

In my very first masters' class at Johns Hopkins, I met a tall, handsome blond man who ranked highly in the Coast Guard. At a class break I found myself sharing my Dad's story and hoping for some answers from a seaman. To my complete surprise, he offered to help me retrieve the incident report from local police, as well as the autopsy results. I quickly provided Dad's name, the date of his death, and his city address in Louisiana.

At my next class I knew why Tall Blonde wanted to help me. He wanted to date me. He went to New York on business and brought me back two scarves – one silk and one cashmere. I hardly knew the man! Out of gratitude I went to dinner with him after class and that's when he shared the reports with me. As I guessed, the police report read as if an eighth grader had written it. A storm raged in the Gulf, the boat was under-manned. No sign of foul play, but the Captain and Dad were the only two on the boat. By law, there should have been a third crewmember. The autopsy showed a blow to the temple, which caused the fall overboard, loss of consciousness and ultimate drowning. Very fishy. And of course, no charges were filed against the Captain, who at the very least had opportunity and ability. As for motive, there was the illegal guns issue…

Had I the resources to pursue the inconsistencies in the report, I would have. Life's treadmill moved me along and I rested in the thought that proving foul play would not bring my father back.

Chapter 24

MARRIAGE, AGAIN

As an undergraduate, I didn't have the self-knowledge to be truly on my own, that is, without a man. So, I did what I do best. I bounced back to Mark. Time and my bad experience with Cookie made it easier for him to forgive me. I wanted so badly for him to experience a world exponentially larger than the Eastern Shore. I enticed and convinced until he gave in and moved to Baltimore to be with me. He got a job at a design firm in a redline neighborhood. I think he was happy with the job and still learning a lot. I know for sure that he hated the city with its smog-belching buses, long lines at the movie theater and melting pot of ethnicities.

He pretended to be content and I ignored his

acting. I guess we were in love again, or still, in spite of my grand detour with Cookie. We tried everything from considering a move out of state to actually getting married. Our faulty reasoning set up a plan for him to go back to his old job in Delaware to acquire the business from his former boss. Then, I was to continue my work at the insurance company, where an internship had proven fruitful, and we would build a home in between.

The Bay Bridge was the in-between, so we chose the least costly side – his. Right after the small wedding, complete with "swanky" reception at the Cambridge Elks, he began construction on our split-level modular home. I was still in our Baltimore apartment and he was staying the workweek at his grandmother's, then toiling evenings on the house.

By this time, Cookie had moved to North Carolina. I hoped that further distance between us would help to cut the (phone) cord. I didn't hate him. I didn't love him anymore. I just felt connected to him in a way I can't explain.

He moved to take a new job but the diabetes precipitated by the pancreatitis and more drinking caused new health complications for him. Heredity also did him no favors. Like his dad, Jack, he developed throat cancer. He was treated with radiation yet kept smoking, switching to Merit and True brands whose claims of less tar were simply marketing jargon. His diabetes worsened from treatment with a pill to daily injections all the while his alcohol intake was modified to rum and Diet Coke, as if this would have a beneficial effect.

During his first hospitalization in North Carolina, his mother Nancy passed away. He called to ask if I would go to her funeral in his stead. Although I hardly knew the woman, after discussing it with Mark, I agreed. I'd like to say I was just being nice, but I did have an ulterior motive – I knew Nancy's brother Harry (the Hollywood producer) would be there. The drive to King of Prussia, Pennsylvania was not very fruitful. I did meet Harry, but the only perk that came of it was a few Christmas cards sent back and forth between us. He was essentially retired and I couldn't really ask him for an audition at his sister's funeral.

Not too long after, everything in everyone's sphere seemed to begin spiraling out, tearing away the dreams of decades past. It was as if the universe was realigning, reshuffling the deck, restacking the logs to create a new order that would be more stable.

I remember calling Mark from the beach house my mom and I had rented. The three generations, grandmother, mother and daughter, were vacationing for a week in Ocean City. I begged him to come down for just a day or two. He refused; his work ethic and devotion to finishing the house too much a priority. It was a blow to our relationship. I begged because emotionally I needed him. I needed him to need me. Years later when he looked back, he realized the error much too late to change events. It was a turning point.

Without Mark to ground me and with Cookie six-hundred plus miles away, I careened from bar to bar and party to party with people I didn't know well. I was searching for an emotional chicken to fill my empty pot.

One of my last dalliances, with a colleague named Brad, turned into a relationship that would be my next episode of looking for Mr. Goodbar and the end of my second stab at marriage. My job was not nearly challenging enough and while I cared about advancing my career, I cared more about being loved. Ironically, Mark loved me in a way that my soul couldn't then comprehend.

I moved into the house that Mark built one week; completely moved out the next. I could not live on the Eastern Shore again. My life was in Baltimore. My future started in Baltimore. I wanted to do plays on the weekends and go to school at night. I couldn't do either if I lived in Stevensville. I won't detail Mark's devastation. It wasn't quite the car into tree scenario; it was angrier. The anger appeared physically in the form of a divorce decree. I was sorry for how we got to this blue-covered document. I just knew I'd never be happy in the long run if I stayed on the Shore. The Force was again driving me, this time away.

Chapter 25

WHERE NOW?

THERE WAS A long hiatus in my contact with Cookie during my relationship with Brad. I had graduated and was busy focusing on my career. Cookie was trying a few work-from-home schemes that never seemed to pan out. He also spent lots of time going in and out of hospitals, so there was the sporadic "I'm dying" call, but I took them none too seriously. Crying wolf was his specialty.

Brad and I worked at the same company and he had admired me from afar for some time. I had no idea. When we hooked up at the cast party for the work-sponsored play we both were in, it was a surprise. I was highly attracted to his lifestyle, his connections, what I perceived as his upward mobility. Or, maybe it was the challenge I loved. He never seemed as close, intimate or in love as I wanted him to be. Could it have had something to do with the fact that when we met, I in my 20s, he in his 30s, that he still lived at home with his mother?

We were friends, lovers and companions but I don't think we were ever destined to be together forever. He, the Gemini, blew hot and cold - mostly cold - and I quickly tired of being treated like leftover Chinese food – stored in the fridge, taken for granted and consumed at his convenience. I say this, but we were a steady item for six years altogether.

I think we gave each other too much freedom. I know that sounds counterintuitive, but a loose grip is best without too much rope to get yourself into trouble. He was a serial monogamist who was not likely to marry and I was still searching for the right balance of love, career and life.

One Christmas, as the finale to gift opening, he tossed a wrapped box across the room at me. I opened it to see a diamond ring that I had chosen at a recent jewelry show. I looked at him, waiting for the question that should have come with it. And, I waited. After the silence and a quiet thanks from me, from that day on, when anyone admired the ring, I would say, "It didn't come with a question."

For the first couple of years we had lots of fun. I

met new people and enjoyed first time experiences like international travel. I really didn't want to get married again but eventually I realized that this status quo was enough for him forever. It was not how I saw my long-term future.

I was pursuing my passion for acting. After rehearsal and publicity photos for the play I was appearing in at Fells Point Corner Theater, the cast and some of the crew went to a bar on Cross Street. I really had no intention of looking for a new love interest, but one found me nonetheless.

I met Stephen in a bar and music venue, 8x10, in south Baltimore during a time when I felt taken for granted by Brad. He followed me out of the bar at 2:00 a.m., knocked on my car window and asked if I wanted to play darts. It was cute, original. I had a big audition the next day for another community theatre play and was struggling with the hour and my caution. I said I wanted to go back into the bar to tell my friends where I was going. He said, "Oh, they'll end up at this party."

His smile convinced me to trust him and he led me down a dark alley to a literal tenement. I admit I was scared. "What the hell are you doing?" I asked myself. Somewhere deep down, The Force must have reassured me. We climbed the rickety steps to the music's point of origin and within thirty seconds I saw a familiar face. It was Elaine's cousin whom I had met a couple of times at her house. Later, a few dart games in, my friends arrived. The fear lifted enough for me to get to know him. I took a big risk that night and luck was on my side. I do not recommend this type of behavior.

Here I was, back in a familiar triangle. I felt guilty seeing Stephen behind Brad's back but I did not let that state of affairs last long. With every moment, I became more and more enthralled with Stephen. First, he was gorgeous – one of the most handsome men I ever dated. Second, he felt his emotions deeply and was not afraid to show them – the antithesis of Brad. And third, it was easy – no work, no walking on eggshells, just being myself. He had no expectation of me and that was a relief. Once I recognized this feeling of freedom, I could see that both Cookie and Brad had wanted me to be something I was not – an ornament for their arm to make them feel "more than."

There were so many coincidences between the lives of Stephen and me it was eerie. He had relatives on the Eastern Shore, as did I. On our second date, I discovered that his cousin and mine had been roommates. Very quickly we were sucked into a deep passion that I had not felt since I first met Mark.

We were happy for a while just being together and not expecting a future. In fact, we never spoke of marriage, although it did come up that he wanted children. This should have been a warning flag for me, yet so enveloping was the physical relationship that it eventually overtook our emotional intimacy. We fell into a living together arrangement that left me on the red side of the financial ledger and I resented that. Money was not important to Stephen and ambition was not his priority.

Seeing Brad at work on a regular basis didn't help my situation. He could tell that I was increasingly unhappy with my financial living arrangement. After several attempts to woo me back, Brad got me to agree to spend time with him. Ugh. Here I was back like that old song, "Torn between Two Lovers." I wanted the emotional love I got from Stephen and the lifestyle I got from Brad. If at all possible, in all circumstances, avoid this situation. It will tear out your heart.

Here's an example of how: Stephen had to work on New Years Eve. He was a waiter at one of Baltimore's top restaurants. Brad wanted to spend the evening with me. I cooked up a story of spending the night on the Eastern Shore with my friend Candy, in order to be with Brad. I stayed the night but didn't have a great time, felt guilty and wanted to just go home (to the apartment I currently shared with Stephen).

It started to snow. I left about a half inch too late. As I drove my Honda Prelude down the on ramp from Dulaney Valley Road to I695, my trusty front wheel drive let me down. I skidded on the ice right into the curbed embankment, knocking my axle apart in the front. I managed to slide the car all the way down under the overpass and close to the shoulder. I was done for and my cover lie luck had run out.

Crying as the snowflakes fell on my cheeks, I waved down an SUV taking the ramp up off 695 and asked for a ride the four blocks back to Brad's house. There was no getting out of this predicament. I could not take a cab (New Year's Day and all); I could not get my car repaired for at least two more days. I was stuck in Towson. I called every one of the friends I could think of, spewing out my problem, but with snow piling up no one could physically come and rescue me. I begged Brad to take me home and he wouldn't. He had won. Nature was on his side. And my decision was made for me.

Once the whole torrid story came out, Stephen was livid and stripped most of his belongings out of the apartment. I have never been so ill from an emotional upset.

I couldn't eat; I couldn't work. Anyone who knows me at all can imagine just how sick I was – I was never too sick to work – ever.

The first week, I did not get out of bed. I called Cookie and poured out my heartbreak in irony as he listened and felt vindicated. My friend Jane came to stay with me toward the end of that week, helping me eat and trying to get me dressed. I just wallowed in how badly I had messed up both relationships. She talked me into an upright position and soon I was eating soup. Still, I pined for Stephen.

On Friday night, Jane called my other friend Missy

and we planned to go out. I was finally well coifed, made up and ready to be seen by the world. I had lost four pounds. I was originally scheduled to go to my grandmother's house that day for the weekend, but I decided to delay my trip til Saturday.

Jane and I were having a glass of wine, waiting for Missy. A metallic sound interrupted our mood, as a key turned in the front door. I ran to the door and flung it open to see Stephen, flummoxed. Before words could erupt, I jumped up on him and wrapped my legs around like a five-year-old. I was clinging so tightly, we both collapsed on the stoop, me sitting on his lap.

"What are you doing here?" he asked. "You're supposed to be at your grandmother's."

"You are supposed to be skiing," I said.

"I didn't go. I came to smell the pillows. I miss you," he admitted.

"I miss you too. And I am soooo sorry. Please stay here. Don't go. I have been a basket case," I pleaded.

Meanwhile, Jane called Missy, who late-as-usual had not left her house. She told Missy the outing was off and promptly excused herself to give us some time alone.

The evening was tearful and melted into the bedroom for what should have been exquisite sexual healing. I know a lot of women pride themselves on their intuition but mine had been on a tear in recent years. I had this nagging feeling that I was not the only one who had decimated the trust that bound us. The Force soon told me he had engaged in revenge sex. He didn't confess it until I made the accusation and knew exactly who it was with – some barfly who hung out where he waited tables. She will remain nameless here, but you know who you are "A."

I believed that our love could withstand my infidelity and he was also hoping. But two wrongs certainly didn't make any of it right and it was soon apparent that what we had was irrevocably destroyed. We tried for a few weeks, but no amount of forgiveness could take us back to the trust bubble we previously enjoyed. We both knew it was really over when he and his brother came over to move his piano.

During this latest upheaval and betrayal, I didn't call Cookie for any more moral support. He was smug and enjoyed my distress a bit too much. I believe this is the first time I mused that our connection might have been on its last legs or even gone. To my surprise, Brad discovered through the work grapevine that I was alone and he called. He forgave me and wanted to try again.

Brad's idea of commitment was moving in together, but I felt no closer to him than before. I pushed for this arrangement because I wanted him to see what it was like to live with someone who was not his mother. Also, it assisted me financially.

I wonder if there is a pledge that some men take to be perennial bachelors? Maybe, but even Warren

Beatty and George Clooney surrendered eventually. Brad was an avid golfer, which meant he spent most of the weekend away from me, and ample time at the nineteenth holes. This relationship was completely the opposite of the one with Stephen. Little intimacy, far too loose a grip and a social calendar lopsided with his friends took equal turns pounding the tiny ember that was left between us.

I also began to notice that his drinking bothered me. I certainly was not a teetotaler and had no right to throw stones. Maturity was dawning in me and I was trying to choose my drinking moments more carefully. I wondered, "What was it with me? Did I have an internal magnet that attracted rum? Was it a throwback to my grandfather? Did I have a problem too?" Unlike Cookie, Brad was always very functional and in control so anyone else may not have registered it as a problem. I had been sensitized by my past, but booze was not the cause of our demise. It was my new Plan B – owning a home by the time I was 30.

Chapter 26

FINDING MR. RIGHT?

THE HOMEOWNERSHIP PLAN B worked out fine, although I had my thirtieth birthday the month before I settled on the house. I moved out of Brad's house without so much as a "please don't go." For whatever reason, we continued to have the occasional date. As a strong planner and goal-oriented implementer, I felt accomplished in purchasing my own home. Emotionally, particularly in my relationships, I was still yearning, searching and unfulfilled.

Now that I was in my own abode, Cookie and I were having more than the occasional phone call, especially when he was sick. He called more when he was in the hospital. I lent a sympathetic ear and he continued to tell me I was the love of his life.

Mark had remarried. I'm not sure why but I tried a third time to rebuild a relationship with Stephen, even after he broke the girlfriend rule and began dating someone I had worked with who called herself my friend. Luckily, I saw her only as an acquaintance and he assured me it was only friendly. During this stab at rekindling the spark, he helped me with a couple of fixes in the new house. The heat still smoldered between us but the trust remained irreparably broken. I had torn it apart by going back to Brad and he could not get over the wound. Despite the revenge sex, the failure was my fault completely.

Between the phone calls, I actually saw Cookie face to face once after I moved into my house. I planned to drive to Greenville to visit an old college friend and mentioned it to Cookie during a call. He was in Raleigh and pleaded to see me so I agreed to a lunch.

His arrival at the restaurant shocked both me and my friend. I hadn't laid eyes on him for years and I knew he was ill, but I wasn't prepared to see him like this. He was emaciated and missing his right leg from the knee down. A combination of diabetes and peripheral artery disease, one caused by alcoholism and one dictated by genetics and smoking, had vandalized his limb. Witnessing this crippled version of him stirred the same emotion as those Humane Society ads that feature abused pets. He beamed as he showed me the devices that made his car safe for him to drive and told me how great it was to see me.

He said he still loved me after all these years. I wondered how this could be the same man who seduced me 15 years earlier. And all I could muster was pity. How do you help someone who won't help himself? I had no clue.

What I finally did know was I couldn't go back to my old pattern between men. I had to change my tactics. I also saw time marching forward and my life was not on the chapter that I had planned.

One of my male cousins was in need of accommodations. The basement of my new townhouse was finished with a full bath and half kitchen. It needed only a stove to be self-contained. He settled in paying a very nominal rent – good for him and help for me when snow needed shoveling or a toilet needed plunging. One Friday night, I played matchmaker and fixed him up with my friend Nina. We all went to Fells Point and landed at the Waterfront Hotel listening to my friend David Zee croon. David is a songwriter, who in addition to his live gigs and recordings, has had a good career scoring video productions.

I complained to Nina about not seeing any good-looking guys, when a stream of them paraded through the front door and past the bar. As the last in line swept by, I said, "See that guy? He's my type."

Nina: "He looks gay."

Me: "No way. You'll see. I'll talk to him before we leave."

People say a bar is not an appropriate place to meet a mate. Well, neither is the Internet but it happens. This was the beginning of the one that stuck, even if he did have two kids.

It took a very long time for us to find ourselves each at the same emotional level as the other. For five years we dated exclusively, as he did the internal work to overcome the emotional wreckage that was his first marriage. He is the type that takes a long time to trust again. I knew this and I was patient – to a point. I was trying a new approach.

As I was not getting any younger, at the aforementioned point I said, enough. Move in or move on. After two weeks of no contact the ache in my gut was just beginning to subside. I had won my tennis match on this particular Wednesday evening and I pulled up in front of the townhouse drenched in sweat but feeling better. I noticed all the lights were on; windows were open. Faint music and the aroma of spaghetti sauce seeped through the screens.

I crossed the front threshold to see two giant suitcases at the bottom of the steps. Jay turned the corner from the kitchen, apron on, and said, "Dinner's ready." I looked at him and pointed to the luggage. He responded with, "You said move in. Here I am."

Once this impasse was crossed, the path to the

eventual legal commitment was smooth. I guess the old adage, "third time's a charm" is true. The only interruptions were those infrequent calls from Cookie to report a new medical problem. He had stopped begging me to see him, most likely because he knew his time was limited and the request futile. Still, he called often and always sent a card on my birthday.

Chapter 27

━━━◥◆◤━━━

ANOTHER BIRTHDAY

THE DAY BEFORE my 36th birthday was uneventful compared to some birthdays past: a normal Friday filled with work, cake with the office crew and last minute errands to prepare and pack. My gift this year was a vacation. Jay's company was sending him to a boondoggle conference and I was tagging along. Not as romantic as I would have liked, but a lot cheaper. And, we were staying an extra week to see the sights.

It had been a long evening, with me packing way too many clothes for my first ever trip to Hawaii. Jay and I were tired and it was past 11 o'clock. Anticipation lingered in the bedroom as we snuggled under the covers but the long flight ahead called for sleep.

The shrieking phone jarred both of us awake. The clock said 12:55 a.m. I answered on the phone by the bed, but as soon as I deciphered that it was Cookie's daughter, Shea, I moved down to the living room. Jay still didn't like it when Cookie continued to intrude into our lives.

"You know Dad was in the hospital," she said. I had momentarily lost track because of his multiple hospitalizations. This time, I wasn't sure which ailment or lifestyle choice was causing the problem. The hard living, smoking and drinking were taking their toll: throat cancer, diabetes, and P.A.D. At 54, he refused to change his habits, continuing to smoke and drink. His stubborn clinging to a lifestyle his body could no longer support had already cost him half a leg.

I remembered that he was hospitalized again because Cookie had called to tell me he was dying. After the third call into the second week, I tended to discount the direness of his condition. With tonight's call, I wished I had taken his warnings seriously.

"He died just a few minutes ago," Shea said. In a split-second, I felt like I was falling backward into the Grand Canyon during an eclipse. I was deaf, mute and blind: in cerebral shock; like the night of my near fatal drug combo. I knew it was true, but my soul couldn't accept it right away. The human connection I had with Cookie for nearly half my life was cut.

For more than twenty minutes as I absorbed the

details from Shea, a debate raged in my head about whether or not to go to him. Some part of me still felt an obligation, but I was leaving for Hawaii. My rational side took over, arguing that he had once again lied to me. I was not, as he had insisted on his last call, his "in case of emergency" person. The hospital obviously had called his daughter instead. Reason shifted into anger – it was just like him to do this! Was he trying to ruin my vacation or the first really happy, stable, faithful relationship I had had in years?

After I very assertively made Shea understand that I would not travel to North Carolina to clean up Cookie's life and collect his ashes, I felt unburdened and more calm. His very long chapter in my life was finally over.

As I sat in the dark something dawned on me. The hospital told Shea that for the past few days Cookie had been conscious but unable to speak and his last call to me had been a few days earlier. Cookie was a tough S.O.B. He knew the date when he went into the hospital. He told me on the phone that he wasn't going home again. Yet he had barely held on until April 8. It was indeed deliberate, if one has any control over these things. He had died on my birthday as a sign to me that in his own twisted way, he cared. It was his way of saying, "remember me and goodbye."

I rose toward the steps but stopped at the hall table and flicked on the table light. A stack of mail from the week sat unopened and unsorted, ready for my flight.

Silently, I flipped through the bills to a couple of birthday cards. It was there. The last one I would ever get from Cookie. I didn't open it.

I heard Jay's voice softly from upstairs, "Are you coming to bed?" as I turned off the light.

Afterword

PEOPLE OFTEN ASK me if I regret my childhood or the significant relationship that made it stand out from the crowd. My answer is no. I felt, as many teens do, that I knew what I was doing and had some degree of control. Cookie was human and made an adult mistake. Who among us hasn't? Some may label it child abuse but I don't. I label it love.

The moral zeitgeist was different in the '70s than today. Scenarios like ours were much more prevalent and if not accepted, then ignored. It took a long time for me to fully mature and be content with my situation. But, I would not trade my teenaged exploits for anything. It has made me, and my life, unique and the experience gives me a different way of looking at a variety of situations in life.

I wish Cookie hadn't been so self destructive so we could still chat about our perspectives now that I'm middle aged. Then again, his behavior, I believe was born of unhappiness and if he were still alive, he'd be miserable. As for me, I don't have any more Plan Bs for my relationships. The only one I have now is for my career. I'm already working on my next book about my best friend's mother's murder. It's going to be killer!